# FREE STUFF FOR KIDS

## Our Pledge

We have collected and examined the best free and up-to-a-dollar offers that we could find (plus a few extra-special over-a-dollar values!). Each supplier in this book has promised to honor properly made requests for **single items** through **1994**. Though mistakes do happen, we are doing our best to make sure this book really works.

**Meadowbrook Press**
Distributed by Simon & Schuster
New York

**The Free Stuff Editors**

**Director:** Bruce Lansky
**Editor/Researcher:** Cathy Broberg
**Managing Editor:** Elizabeth Weiss
**Production Manager:** Kate Laing
**Desktop Publishing Coordinator:** Jon C. Wright
**Designer:** Tabor Harlow

ISBN: 0-88166-202-X
Simon & Schuster Ordering #: 0-671-87286-9

ISSN: 1056-9693
17th edition

Published by Meadowbrook Press, 18318 Minnetonka Boulevard, Deephaven, MN 55391.

BOOK TRADE DISTRIBUTION by Simon & Schuster, a division of Simon and Schuster, Inc., 1230 Avenue of the Americas, New York, NY 10020.

93 94   5 4 3 2 1

Printed in the United States of America

# Contents

# Thank You's

To Pat Blakely, Barbara Haislet, and Judith Hentges for creating and publishing the original *Rainbow Book,* and for proving that kids, parents, and teachers would respond enthusiastically to a source of free things by mail. They taught us the importance of carefully checking the quality of each item and doing our best to make sure that each and every request is satisfied.

Our heartfelt appreciation goes to hundreds of organizations and individuals for making this book possible. The suppliers and editors of this book have a common goal: to make it possible for kids to reach out and discover the world by themselves.

MEADOWBROOK PRESS
1994
EDITION

U.S.
MAIL

# USING THIS BOOK

# About This Book

*Free Stuff for Kids* contains listings of hundreds of items to send away for. The Free Stuff Editors have examined every item and think they're among the best offers available. There are no trick offers—only safe, fun, and informative things you'll like!

This book is designed for kids who can read and write. The directions in **Using This Book** explain exactly how to request an item. Read the instructions carefully so you know how to send a request. Making sure you've filled out a request correctly is easy—just complete the *Free Stuff for Kids* Checklist on p. 8. Half the fun is using the book on your own. The other half is getting a real reward for your efforts!

Each year the Free Stuff Editors create a new edition of this book, taking out old items, inserting new ones, and changing addresses and prices. It is important for you to use an updated edition because the suppliers only honor properly made requests for single items for the **current** edition. If you use this edition after **1994,** your request might not be honored.

## Getting Your Book in Shape

Before sending for free stuff, get your book in shape. Fold it open one page at a time, working from the two ends toward the middle. This will make the book lie flat when you read or copy addresses.

## Reading Carefully

Read the descriptions of the offers carefully to find out exactly what you're getting. Here are some guidelines to help you know what you're sending for:

• A pamphlet or foldout is usually one sheet of paper folded over and printed on both sides.

• A booklet is usually larger and contains more pages, but it's smaller than a book.

## Following Directions

It's important to follow each supplier's directions. On one offer, you might need to use a postcard. On another offer, you might be asked to include money or a long self-addressed, stamped envelope. If you do not follow the directions **exactly,** you might not get your request. Ask for only **one** of anything you send for. Family or classroom members using the same book must send separate requests.

## Sending Postcards

A postcard is a small card you can write on and send through the mail without an envelope. Many suppliers offering free items require you to send requests on postcards. Please do this. It saves them the time it takes to open many envelopes.

The post office sells postcards with pre-printed postage. The cost of these postcards is 19¢. You can also buy postcards at a drugstore and put stamps on them yourself. (Postcards with a picture on them are usually more expensive.) You must use a postcard that is at least 3½ by 5½ inches. (The post office will not take 3-by-5-inch index cards.) Your postcards should be addressed like the one below.

Jessie Rogers
2415 Lake Street
Solon Springs, WI 54873

USA 19

Fan Pack
Detroit Tigers
Tiger Stadium
Detroit, MI 48216

Dear Sir or Madam:

Please send me a Detroit Tigers fan pack.

Thank you very much.

Sincerely,
Jessie Rogers

2415 Lake Street
Solon Springs, WI 54873

- **Neatly print** the supplier's address on the side of the postcard that has the postage. Put your return address in the upper left-hand corner of that side as well.
- **Neatly print** your request, your name, and your address on the blank side of the postcard.
- Do not abbreviate the name of your street or city.
- Use a ballpoint pen.

# Sending Letters

Your letters should look like the one below.

- **Neatly print** the name of the item you want exactly as you see it in the directions.
- **Neatly print** your own name and address at the bottom of the letter. (Do not abbreviate the name of your street or city.)
- If you're including coins or a long self-addressed, stamped envelope, say so in the letter.
- Put a first-class stamp (they cost 29¢) on any envelope you send. You can get stamps at the post office.
- **Neatly print** the supplier's address in the center of the envelope and your return address in the upper left-hand corner.
- If you're sending many letters at once, make sure you put the right letter in the right envelope.
- Use a ballpoint pen. Pencil can be difficult to read, and ink pen often smears.

## Sending a Long Self-Addressed, Stamped Envelope

If the directions say to enclose a long self-addressed, stamped envelope, here's how to do it:

• **Neatly print** your name and address in the center of a 9½-inch long envelope as if you were mailing it to yourself. Print your return address in the upper left-hand corner of the envelope as well. Put a first-class stamp on it.

• Fold up (but don't seal!) the long self-addressed, stamped envelope, and put it inside another 9½-inch long envelope (along with your letter to the supplier) and put a first-class stamp on it.

• **Neatly print** the supplier's address in the center of the envelope you are sending and your return address in the upper left-hand corner.

• Use a ballpoint pen.

## Sending Money

Many of the suppliers in this book are not charging you for their items. However, the cost of postage and handling is high today, and suppliers must charge you for this. If the directions say to enclose money for postage and handling, you must do so. Here are a few rules about sending money:

• Tape the coins to your letter so they won't break out of the envelope.

• Don't stack your coins on top of each other in the envelope.

• If an item costs $1.00, send a one-dollar bill instead of coins. Don't tape dollar bills.

• Send only U.S. money.

• If a grown-up is helping you, he/she may write a check (unless the directions say otherwise).

• Send all money directly to the suppliers—their addresses are listed with their offers.

## Getting Your Free Stuff

Expect to wait four to eight weeks for your free stuff to arrive. Sometimes you have to wait longer. Remember, suppliers get thousands of requests each year. Please be patient! If you wait a long time and your offer still doesn't come, you may be using the wrong edition. This is the **1994** edition—the offers in this book will only be good for 1993 and 1994!

## Making Sure You Get Your Request

The Free Stuff Editors have tried to make the directions for using this book as clear as possible to make sure you get what you send for. But you must follow **all** of the directions **exactly** as they're written, or the supplier will not be able to answer your request. If you're confused about the directions, ask a grown-up to help you.

## Do's and Don'ts:

- **Do** use a ballpoint pen.
- **Do** print. Cursive can be difficult to read.
- **Do** print your name, address, and zip code clearly and fully on the postcard or on the envelope **and** the letter you send. Do not abbreviate anything except state names. Abbreviations can be confusing, and sometimes envelopes and letters get separated after they reach the supplier.
- **Do** send the correct amount of U.S. money, but use as few coins as possible.
- **Do** tape the coins you send to the letter you send them with. If you don't, the money might rip the envelope and fall out.
- **Do** use a 9½-inch long self-addressed, stamped envelope if the instructions say you should.

- **Do not** ask for more than **one** of an item.
- **Do not** stack coins in the envelope.
- **Do not** seal your long self-addressed, stamped envelope. The suppliers need to be able to put the item you ordered in the envelope you send.
- **Do not** ask Meadowbrook Press to send you any of the items listed in the book unless you are ordering the Meadowbrook offers from p. 37, p. 38, or p. 39. The publishers of this book do not carry items belonging to other suppliers. They do not supply refunds, either.

**Follow all the rules to avoid disappointment!**

## What to Do If You Aren't Satisfied:

If you have complaints about any offer, or if you don't receive the items you sent for within eight to ten weeks, contact the Free Stuff Editors. Before you complain, please reread the directions. Are you sure you followed them properly? Are you using this **1994** edition **after** 1994? (Offers here are only good for 1993 and 1994.) The Free Stuff Editors won't be able to send you the item, but they can make sure that any suppliers who don't fulfill requests are dropped from next year's *Free Stuff for Kids*. We'd like to know which offers you like and what kind of new offers you'd like us to add to next year's edition. So don't be bashful—write us a letter. Send your complaints or suggestions to:

The Free Stuff Editors
Meadowbrook Press
18318 Minnetonka Boulevard
Deephaven, MN 55391

# *Free Stuff for Kids* Checklist

Use this checklist each time you send out a request. It will help you follow directions exactly and prevent mistakes. Put a check mark in the box each time you complete a task—you can photocopy this page and use it again and again.

**When sending postcards and letters:**

❑ I used a ballpoint pen.

❑ I printed neatly and carefully.

❑ I asked for the correct item (only one).

❑ I wrote to the correct supplier.

❑ I double-checked the supplier's address.

**When sending postcards only:**

❑ I put my return address on the postcard.

❑ I applied a 19¢ stamp (if the postage wasn't pre-printed).

**When sending letters only:**

❑ I put my return address on the letter.

❑ I included a long self-addressed, stamped envelope (if the directions asked for one).

❑ I included the correct amount of money (if the directions asked for money).

❑ I put my return address on the envelope.

❑ I applied a 29¢ stamp.

**When sending a long self-addressed, stamped envelope:**

❑ I used a 9½-inch long envelope.

❑ I put my address on the front of the envelope.

❑ I put my return address in the upper left-hand corner of the envelope.

❑ I left the envelope unsealed.

❑ I applied a 29¢ stamp.

**When sending a one-dollar bill:**

❑ I sent U.S. money.

❑ I enclosed a one-dollar bill with my letter instead of coins.

**When sending coins:**

❑ I sent U.S. money.

❑ I taped the coins to my letter.

❑ I did not stack the coins on top of each other.

# SPORTS

# Go Twins

Play ball! The Minnesota Twins have an offer you won't want to miss. Send for a schedule, brochure, and photo packet (depending on availability) from the team that finished second in the American League West in 1992.

| Directions: | Write your request on paper, and put it in an envelope. You must enclose a long self-addressed, stamped envelope. |
|---|---|
| Write to: | Fan Mail<br>Minnesota Twins<br>501 Chicago Avenue South<br>Minneapolis, MN 55415 |
| Ask for: | Minnesota Twins pocket schedule, novelty brochure, and team/player photos |

# Sock It to 'em

White Sox fans, here's an offer for you! This sticker features the logo of the team with All-Star players like Bo Jackson, Frank Thomas, and Robin Ventura.

| Directions: | Write your request on paper, and put it in an envelope. You must enclose a long self-addressed, stamped envelope. |
|---|---|
| Write to: | Chicago White Sox<br>333 West 35th Street<br>Chicago, IL 60616 |
| Ask for: | Chicago White Sox logo sticker |

# Yankee Doodle Dandy

Batter up! One of the American League's oldest teams has an offer you'll want to swing at. Send for a New York Yankees bumper sticker, schedule, and decal (depending on availability).

| **Directions:** | Write your request on paper, and put it in an envelope. You must enclose a long self-addressed, stamped envelope. |
|---|---|
| **Write to:** | Community Relations Department c/o Tom Paulson New York Yankees Yankee Stadium Bronx, NY 10451 |
| **Ask for:** | New York Yankees bumper sticker, pocket schedule, and decal |

# They're G-r-r-r-eat!

This pitch is right down the pipe! The Detroit Tigers fan pack includes a team sticker and schedule. You'll also get a photo of a team member or manager Sparky Anderson, the legendary skipper of the Tigers (depending on availability).

| **Directions:** | Write your request on paper, and put it in an envelope. You must enclose a long self-addressed, stamped envelope. |
|---|---|
| **Write to:** | Fan Pack Detroit Tigers Tiger Stadium Detroit, MI 48216 |
| **Ask for:** | Detroit Tigers fan pack |

**BASEBALL**

# Catch the Spirit

Have you ever heard of the Green Monster? You can see it at Fenway Park in Boston. This Red Sox fan pack includes a brochure, pocket schedule, and player postcard (depending on availability). You'll also get information on how you can join the Coca-Cola Rookie Red Sox fan club and the Fenway Park tours.

| Directions: | Write your request on paper, and put it in an envelope. You must enclose an 8-by-10-inch self-addressed, stamped envelope. |
|---|---|
| Write to: | Red Sox Fan Stuff<br>4 Yawkey Way<br>Boston, MA 02215 |
| Ask for: | Boston Red Sox brochure, pocket schedule, player postcard, and fan information |

# Root for the Rangers

St-eee-rike! Cheer on the team that calls the Lone Star state home. This Texas Rangers fan pack includes a team schedule, logo sticker, and souvenir list (depending on availability).

| Directions: | Write your request on paper, and put it in an envelope. You must enclose a long self-addressed, stamped envelope. |
|---|---|
| Write to: | Texas Rangers Souvenirs<br>P.O. Box 90111<br>Arlington, TX 76004-3111 |
| Ask for: | Texas Rangers schedule, sticker, and souvenir list |

# Amazing Astros

The Houston Astros, named in honor of the astronauts and the nearby Johnson Space Center, have a great offer for baseball fans. Their fan pack features a schedule, logo sticker, and player photo (depending on availability).

| **Directions:** | Write your request on paper, and put it in an envelope. You must enclose a long self-addressed, stamped envelope. |
|---|---|
| **Write to:** | Houston Astros Public Relations P.O. Box 288 Houston, TX 77001-0288 |
| **Ask for:** | Houston Astros schedule, logo sticker, and player photo |

# Hall of Fame

Fans of all Major League teams can enjoy this offer from the Baseball Hall of Fame. You'll get a shiny Baseball Hall of Fame decal and gift catalog.

| **Directions:** | Write your request on paper, and put it in an envelope. You must enclose **$1.00.** |
|---|---|
| **Write to:** | National Baseball Hall of Fame Decal Offer P.O. Box 590A Cooperstown, NY 13326 |
| **Ask for:** | Baseball Hall of Fame decal and catalog |

# Red Hot!

Celebrate the hottest game on ice. Send for this fan pack from the Detroit Red Wings, and you'll get a team photo, schedule, and merchandise catalog (depending on availability).

| | |
|---|---|
| **Directions:** | Write your request on paper, and put it in an envelope. You must enclose a long self-addressed, stamped envelope. |
| **Write to:** | Detroit Red Wings<br>600 Civic Center Drive<br>Detroit, MI 48226 |
| **Ask for:** | Detroit Red Wings fan pack |

# A Capital Idea

"Caps" fans will love this offer from the Washington Capitals. Their fan pack includes team information sheets, a schedule, a souvenir brochure, and a bumper sticker (depending on availability).

| | |
|---|---|
| **Directions:** | Write your request on paper, and put it in an envelope. You must enclose a long self-addressed, stamped envelope. |
| **Write to:** | Washington Capitals<br>Capital Centre<br>Landover, MD 20785<br>Attention: Fan Mail |
| **Ask for:** | Washington Capitals fan pack |

# Hit the Ice

Luge is the French word for sled. This exciting winter sport has been a part of the Olympics since 1964. You can learn more about lugers and their sleds by sending for this pamphlet.

| Directions: | Write your request on paper, and put it in an envelope. You must enclose a long self-addressed, stamped envelope. |
|---|---|
| Write to: | U.S. Luge Association<br>P.O. Box 651<br>Lake Placid, NY 12946 |
| Ask for: | Luge pamphlet |

# Slide on Down

Bobsled and Skeleton athletes race down icy bobsled tracks on special sleds. Bobsled sliders race in teams of two and four, but only one person rides on a Skeleton sled. Find out more about Bobsled and Skeleton in this pamphlet. You'll also get a Bobsled window decal.

SUPPORTING

UNITED STATES
BOBSLED & SKELETON
FEDERATION

| Directions: | Write your request on paper, and put it in an envelope. You must enclose a long self-addressed, stamped envelope and **$1.00**. |
|---|---|
| Write to: | U.S. Bobsled and Skeleton Federation<br>Box 828<br>Lake Placid, NY 12946 |
| Ask for: | Shoot the Wall pamphlet and U.S. Bobsled decal |

# Ski and Shoot

The biathlon is a winter Olympic sport that combines cross-country skiing and target shooting. It comes from the Scandinavian countries, but the United States also has a biathlon team. You can show your support for them by displaying this decal.

| Directions: | Write your request on paper, and put it in an envelope. You must enclose **$1.00.** |
| --- | --- |
| Write to: | U.S. Biathlon Association<br>Logo Sales<br>P.O. Box 859<br>West Farmington, ME 04992 |
| Ask for: | U.S. Biathlon team decal |

# Good as Gold

Dive right into this offer! The U.S. Swimming competition isn't just about going for the gold—it's about building a tradition that's as good as gold. Get this decal, and show your support.

| Directions: | Write your request on paper, and put it in an envelope. You must enclose a long self-addressed, stamped envelope. |
| --- | --- |
| Write to: | United States Swimming<br>Marketing Department<br>One Olympic Plaza<br>Colorado Springs, CO 80909 |
| Ask for: | United States Swimming logo decal |

# En Garde!

You might be familiar with fencing—the art of sword fighting—from the stories of the Three Musketeers, Robin Hood, and Peter Pan. But did you know that fencing is a popular Olympic sport today? Send for this brochure to learn about fencing's finer points.

| Directions: | Write your request on paper, and put it in an envelope. You must enclose a long self-addressed, stamped envelope. |
|---|---|
| Write to: | USFA<br>Promotional Department<br>1750 East Boulder Street<br>Colorado Springs, CO 80909-5774 |
| Ask for: | Spectator Brochure |

# Foiled Again!

Get this colorful United States Fencing Association decal, and show that you support young fencers who hope to enter the Olympics one day.

| Directions: | Write your request on paper, and put it in an envelope. You must enclose a long self-addressed, stamped envelope and 50¢. |
|---|---|
| Write to: | USFA<br>Promotional Department<br>1750 East Boulder Street<br>Colorado Springs, CO 80909-5774 |
| Ask for: | Fencing decal |

# Soccer Skills

Kids all over the world love to play soccer. This illustrated poster gives you tips to improve your game. You'll also get a colorful patch to wear on your jacket.

| Directions: | Write your request on paper, and put it in an envelope. You must enclose a long self-addressed, stamped envelope and **$1.00.** |
|---|---|
| **Write to:** | Say Soccer<br>Suite #1<br>4903 Vine Street<br>Cincinnati, OH 45217 |
| **Ask for:** | Soccer skills poster and SAY USA soccer patch |

# Practical Pedaling

Mountain biking is a super way to exercise and have fun. Knowing a few simple rules of the trail will help keep mountain biking safe for everyone. This pamphlet shows you how to ride responsibly.

CONTROL YOUR BICYCLE!

| Directions: | Write your request on paper, and put it in an envelope. You must enclose a long self-addressed, stamped envelope and **25¢.** |
|---|---|
| **Write to:** | IMBA<br>P.O. Box 412043<br>Los Angeles, CA 91103 |
| **Ask for:** | Wild Willy pamphlet |

# Get Fit!

Arnold Schwarzenegger wants to help you get physically fit. Take the Presidential Sports Award challenge by participating in sports ranging from football to ice-skating. Find out about all the cool awards you can receive if you succeed. (For ages 6 and up.)

| Directions: | Write your request on paper, and put it in an envelope. You must enclose a long self-addressed, stamped envelope. |
|---|---|
| Write to: | Presidential Sports Award Department KI P.O. Box 68207 Indianapolis, IN 46268 |
| Ask for: | Presidential Sports Award pamphlet |

# Get into Lacrosse!

Go for the goal with this exciting magazine from the Lacrosse Foundation. *Lacrosse* will explain everything from "cradling" to who's who in the sport.

| Directions: | Write your request on paper, and put it in an envelope. You must enclose **$1.00.** |
|---|---|
| Write to: | The Lacrosse Foundation 113 West University Parkway Baltimore, MD 21210 |
| Ask for: | *Lacrosse* magazine sample |

# Water Skiing Is Wild!

Giving the thumbs-down sign when you're water skiing doesn't mean you're not having a good time—it signals the boat driver to slow down. Learn more about proper signaling and safety from this illustrated booklet.

| **Directions:** | Write your request on paper, and put it in an envelope. You must enclose a long self-addressed, stamped envelope. |
|---|---|
| **Write to:** | American Water Ski Association<br>799 Overlook Drive<br>Winter Haven, FL 33884 |
| **Ask for:** | Guide to Safe Water Skiing booklet |

# Right up Your Alley

Do you know how to pick out a bowling ball according to your weight, or how to take a four-step approach? This foldout shows you how to do both and more!

**FUN-DAMENTALS
OF BOWLING**

| **Directions:** | Write your request on paper, and put it in an envelope. You must enclose a long self-addressed, stamped envelope. |
|---|---|
| **Write to:** | Young American Bowling Alliance<br>5301 South 76th Street<br>Greendale, WI 53129 |
| **Ask for:** | Bif's Fun-Damentals of Bowling foldout |

# Derby Days

On your mark, get set, go! Get the latest Official All-American Soap Box Derby Activities Book, and learn about entering contests and winning soap box derbies.

| Directions: | Use a postcard. | |
|---|---|---|
| **Write to:** | All-American Soap Box Derby<br>P. O. Box 7233<br>Akron, OH 44306 | |
| **Ask for:** | The Official All-American Soap Box<br>Derby Activities Book | |

# Lost and Found

Orienteering is finding your way, using only a map and compass, along an unknown stretch of ground. It's a challenging way to learn about the land, nature, and yourself. This booklet and sample topographic map will help you get started.

| Directions: | Write your request on paper, and put it in an envelope. You must enclose a long self-addressed, stamped envelope with **two 29¢** stamps. |
|---|---|
| **Write to:** | Silva Orienteering Services, USA<br>Department FS<br>P. O. Box 1604<br>Binghamton, NY 13902 |
| **Ask for:** | Orienteering map and booklet |

# Get Hooked!

Get hooked on fishing. If you love fishing, you'll love this decal. Stick it on your tackle box or notebook to let others know that you're into drug-free activities.

| Directions: | Write your request on paper, and put it in an envelope. You must enclose a long self-addressed, stamped envelope. |
|---|---|
| Write to: | Future Fisherman Foundation<br>Suite 300<br>1250 Grove Avenue<br>Barrington, IL 60010<br>Attention: Kids Stuff |
| Ask for: | Hooked on Fishing decal |

# Fishing Fun

Want to reel in a big fish next time you go fishing? Learn about knots, tackle, and fishing safety with this booklet.

| Directions: | Write your request on paper, and put it in an envelope. You must enclose **$1.00.** |
|---|---|
| Write to: | Future Fisherman Foundation<br>Suite 300<br>1250 Grove Avenue<br>Barrington, IL 60010<br>Attention: Kids Stuff |
| Ask for: | Fishing Fun for Kids booklet |

MEADOWBROOK PRESS
1994 EDITION

U.S. MAIL

# STICKERS

*FREE*

# Fun Food

Feeling hungry? These rainbow-colored sticker sheets feature all your favorite fast foods and desserts. You'll get two sheets.

# Enjoy Coca-Cola

"Trink Coca-Cola" is German for "Drink Coca-Cola." This sticker postcard features the Coke trademark in six different foreign languages, including German, Russian, and Chinese.

Germany

| **Directions:** | Write your request on paper, and put it in an envelope. You must enclose a long self-addressed, stamped envelope and **$1.00.** |
|---|---|
| **Write to:** | Marlene Monroe<br>Department F<br>6210 Ridge Manor Drive<br>Memphis, TN 38115-3411 |
| **Ask for:** | Food stickers |

| **Directions:** | Use a postcard. |
|---|---|
| **Write to:** | Coca-Cola U.S.A.<br>Consumer Information Center<br>Department FS<br>P.O. Drawer 1734<br>Atlanta, GA 30301 |
| **Ask for:** | Coca-Cola sticker postcard (*limit* **one** *per request*) |

# Grand Slam

Hey, baseball fans! Now you can show your support for your favorite teams with these collector sticker packs. Each sticker pack features eight colorful stickers, and you can choose any Major League team—even the new Colorado Rockies and Florida Marlins! (Be sure to specify which baseball team's sticker pack you want.)

| | |
|---|---|
| **Directions:** | Write your request on paper, and put it in an envelope. You must enclose **$1.50**. *(We think this offer is a good value for the money.)* |
| **Write to:** | Mr. Rainbows<br>Department K-14<br>P.O. Box 387<br>Avalon, NJ 08202 |
| **Ask for:** | Baseball team sticker pack *(specify the team you want)* |

# Gorgeous Gems

These shiny stones may look like jewelry, but they're actually stickers. You can stick them on your ears, fingernails, face, or anywhere else. You'll get eight stick-on-stones.

| **Directions:** | Write your request on paper, and put it in an envelope. You must enclose a long self-addressed, stamped envelope and **$1.00.** |
|---|---|
| **Write to:** | The Complete Traveler<br>Department S<br>490 Route 46 East<br>Fairfield, NJ 07004 |
| **Ask for:** | Stick-on-stones |

# Rainbow Colors

Brighten up your sticker collection with these iridescent stickers. Choose from cats, dinosaurs, fish, musical notes, airplanes, or hearts. Pick any two different sheets.

| **Directions:** | Write your request on paper, and put it in an envelope. You must enclose **$1.00.** |
|---|---|
| **Write to:** | Lightning Enterprises<br>P.O. Box 16121<br>West Palm Beach, FL 33416 |
| **Ask for:** | Iridescent sticker sheets |

# Prism Power

Hop to it! These colorful stickers bend the light so that they shine like a prism. This sheet features lots of cute rabbits.

# Happenin' Holograms

When the light hits these hologram stickers, watch the 3-D rainbow effect! You'll get four large stickers featuring wild animals.

| | |
|---|---|
| **Directions:** | Write your request on paper, and put it in an envelope. You must enclose a long self-addressed, stamped envelope and **$1.00.** |
| **Write to:** | Expressions<br>Department RS<br>P.O. Box 18090<br>Boulder, CO 80308-1090 |
| **Ask for:** | Prism rabbits |

| | |
|---|---|
| **Directions:** | Write your request on paper, and put it in an envelope. You must enclose a long self-addressed, stamped envelope and **$1.00.** |
| **Write to:** | Expressions<br>Department HS<br>P.O. Box 18090<br>Boulder, CO 80308-1090 |
| **Ask for:** | Four hologram stickers |

# Cowabunga!

Are you a big fan of Leonardo, Michaelangelo, Raphael, and Donatello; Mario and Luigi; Barbie and Ken; or Fred and Barney? These big, colorful sticker sheets feature all your favorite characters.

| | |
|---|---|
| **Directions:** | Write your request on paper, and put it in an envelope. You must enclose a long self-addressed, stamped envelope and **$1.00** for **each** sheet you request. |
| **Write to:** | Mr. Rainbows<br>Department 2074<br>P.O. Box 387<br>Avalon, NJ 08202 |
| **Ask for:** | • Teenage Mutant Ninja Turtles sticker sheet<br>• Super Mario Brothers sticker sheet<br>• Barbie and Ken sticker sheet<br>• Flintstones sticker sheet |

# Holy Decals, Batman!

Sok! Biff! Kapow! America's caped crusader is here! This sticker sheet features the amazing Batman in five different crime-fighting poses, the famous "Bat Signal," and a few scary bats, too.

# Caped Crusader

Spring into action with these super big, super colorful trading card stickers starring your favorite superhero, Batman. Collect them, display them, or trade them with your friends.

| **Directions:** | Write your request on paper, and put it in an envelope. You must enclose a long self-addressed, stamped envelope and **$1.00.** |
|---|---|
| **Write to:** | Mr. Rainbows<br>Department P-54<br>P.O. Box 387<br>Avalon, NJ 08202 |
| **Ask for:** | Batman sticker sheet |

| **Directions:** | Write your request on paper, and put it in an envelope. You must enclose a long self-addressed, stamped envelope and **$1.00.** |
|---|---|
| **Write to:** | Mr. Rainbows<br>Department P-64<br>P.O. Box 387<br>Avalon, NJ 08202 |
| **Ask for:** | Two Batman trading card stickers |

# Sticker Surprise

If you love to collect all kinds of stickers, here's an offer for you. You'll get a variety of stickers, such as animals, rainbows, musical notes, and more—ten in all! It's a surprise which ones you'll get.

| **Directions:** | Write your request on paper, and put it in an envelope. You must enclose a long self-addressed, stamped envelope and **$1.00.** |
|---|---|
| **Write to:** | Della Kay Castiglione<br>Department 1<br>304 South Hard Road<br>Benld, IL 62009 |
| **Ask for:** | Ten stickers |

# Sunshine State

Florida is known for its bright sunny weather. Send for this mini bumper sticker that reflects light to brighten up your day.

| **Directions:** | Write your request on paper, and put it in an envelope. You must enclose a long self-addressed, stamped envelope and **50¢.** |
|---|---|
| **Write to:** | Parker Flags & Pennants<br>Suite 4<br>5746 Plunkett Street<br>Hollywood, FL 33023-2346 |
| **Ask for:** | Florida mini bumper sticker |

# Glow in the Dark

By day they look like ordinary stickers; by night they have a mysterious glow! These ghoulish and goofy glow-in-the-dark stickers will add a spooky shine to your collection. You'll get one sheet with critters and one with moons.

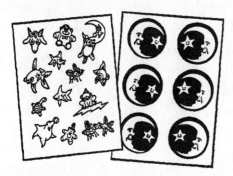

| Directions: | Write your request on paper, and put it in an envelope. You must enclose a long self-addressed, stamped envelope and **$1.00.** |
|---|---|
| **Write to:** | Mr. Rainbows<br>Department P-C4<br>P.O. Box 387<br>Avalon, NJ 08202 |
| **Ask for:** | Glow-in-the-dark critters and moons |

# Fuzzy Animals

These colorful animal stickers are soft and fuzzy—just like real animals! Choose from pets like cats, dogs, or guinea pigs; farm animals like cows, goats, or pigs; or wild animals like raccoons, seals, or koala bears. Pick any two different animal sheets.

| Directions: | Write your request on paper, and put it in an envelope. You must enclose a long self-addressed, stamped envelope and **$1.00.** |
|---|---|
| **Write to:** | Mr. Rainbows<br>Department P-44<br>P.O. Box 387<br>Avalon, NJ 08202 |
| **Ask for:** | Fuzzy animal stickers (*pick any two animals*) |

# Animal Alert!

These shiny animal stickers will add pizzazz to your sticker collection. You'll get one sheet with cats, one with dogs, and one with bears.

| Directions: | Write your request on paper, and put it in an envelope. You must enclose a long self-addressed, stamped envelope and **$1.00.** |
|---|---|
| **Write to:** | Marlene Monroe<br>Department A<br>6210 Ridge Manor Drive<br>Memphis, TN 38115-3411 |
| **Ask for:** | Animal stickers |

# Give the Earth a Hug!

Show everyone that you care about the environment. These fuzzy stickers feature teddy bears hugging the earth.

| Directions: | Write your request on paper, and put it in an envelope. You must enclose a long self-addressed, stamped envelope and **$1.00.** |
|---|---|
| **Write to:** | Mr. Rainbows<br>Department P-24<br>P.O. Box 387<br>Avalon, NJ 08202 |
| **Ask for:** | Fuzzy earth stickers |

MEADOWBROOK PRESS
1994 EDITION

U.S. MAIL

# READING

# Tons of Titles

Can't decide which books to read? Sometimes it's hard to choose from the large number of books in libraries and bookstores. This pamphlet lists more than 100 of the best recent children's books to help you find a favorite.

| **Directions:** | Write your request on paper, and put it in an envelope. You must enclose **$1.00.** |
|---|---|
| **Write to:** | Consumer Information Center Department 101Z Pueblo, CO 81009 |
| **Ask for:** | Books for Children pamphlet |

# Mark Your Place

You'll never lose your place if you mark your page with a bookmark. Here are two colorful satin bookmarks with gold lettering that remind you to "READ READ READ."

| **Directions:** | Write your request on paper, and put it in an envelope. You must enclose a long self-addressed, stamped envelope and **$1.00.** |
|---|---|
| **Write to:** | Fax Marketing Department R 460 Carrollton Drive Frederick, MD 21701-6357 |
| **Ask for:** | READ bookmarks |

# Chipmunk Cheer

Join your favorite cartoon characters by giving a great big cheer for books. You'll get two bookmarks featuring the Chipmunks and Chipettes, plus a plastic Chipmunk book bag for carrying all of your favorite books.

| | |
|---|---|
| **Directions:** | Write your request on paper, and put it in an envelope. You must enclose a long self-addressed, stamped envelope and **$1.00.** |
| **Write to:** | Ann Cummings<br>Department 3<br>106C Witten Circle<br>Havelock, NC 28532 |
| **Ask for:** | Chipmunk bookmarks and book bag |

# Book Care

Treat your books with care, and they'll last a long time. These four bookmarks give you tips on how to care for books. You'll also get a "Read Around the House" plastic book bag to protect your books from the rain and snow.

| | |
|---|---|
| **Directions:** | Write your request on paper, and put it in an envelope. You must enclose a long self-addressed, stamped envelope and **$1.00.** |
| **Write to:** | Ann Cummings<br>Department 4<br>106C Witten Circle<br>Havelock, NC 28532 |
| **Ask for:** | Book-savers bookmarks and book bag |

# Join the Team

It feels great to be part of a winning team. Reading is a "sport" that exercises your mind. Be a reading athlete and wear this button with pride. You can request this U.S.A. button or one featuring your home state.

| Directions: | Write your request on paper, and put it in an envelope. You must enclose **$1.00.** |
|---|---|
| **Write to:** | Ann Cummings<br>Department 1<br>106C Witten Circle<br>Havelock, NC 28532 |
| **Ask for:** | Reading Team button (*specify if you want the U.S.A. button or a state button*) |

# Befriend a Book

Do you love to read? Now you can show off your affection for books by wearing this button.

| Directions: | Write your request on paper, and put it in an envelope. You must enclose **$1.00.** |
|---|---|
| **Write to:** | Ann Cummings<br>Department 2<br>106C Witten Circle<br>Havelock, NC 28532 |
| **Ask for:** | Hug a Book button |

# Fabulous Frogs

Leap into reading with these colorful frog bookmarks. You'll learn how the Tomato frog got its name, how far the Gliding frog can glide, how frogs drink water, and other fun frog facts.

**Directions:** Write your request on paper, and put it in an envelope. You must enclose a long self-addressed, stamped envelope and **50¢** for **each** bookmark you request.

| **Write to:** | The Frog Pond |
| | Department K |
| | P.O. Box 193 |
| | Beech Grove, IN 46107 |

| **Ask for:** | • Gliding frog bookmark |
| | • Tomato frog bookmark |

# Mother Goose Fun

Have you ever heard of the three *kind* mice or the old woman who lived in a *sandal?* You can read about these characters in *The New Adventures of Mother Goose.* This colorful bookmark features some funny new rhymes.

**Directions:** Write your request on paper, and put it in an envelope. You must enclose a long self-addressed, stamped envelope.

| **Write to:** | Meadowbrook Press |
| | Department NMG |
| | 18318 Minnetonka Boulevard |
| | Deephaven, MN 55391 |

| **Ask for:** | New Mother Goose bookmark |

# Storybook Poster

Now you can really make your bedroom look beautiful. Send for this colorful poster featuring your favorite storybook characters, like Corduroy and Curious George. You'll also get a catalog of videos based on award-winning children's books, where these characters come alive!

| Directions: | Write your request on paper, and put it in an envelope. You must enclose **$1.00.** |
|---|---|
| **Write to:** | Children's Circle<br>Department FS4<br>389 Newtown Turnpike<br>Weston, CT 06883 |
| **Ask for:** | "Where Books Come Alive" poster and catalog |

# Betcha Laugh

Who says poetry can't be fun? *Kids Pick the Funniest Poems* is an illustrated book full of hilarious poems chosen by kids your age—you'll find your favorite poets in it! Send for this pamphlet featuring eight of the poems in the book, and get ready to laugh out loud.

| Directions: | Write your request on paper, and put it in an envelope. You must enclose a long self-addressed, stamped envelope and **25¢.** |
|---|---|
| **Write to:** | Meadowbrook Press<br>Department FP<br>18318 Minnetonka Boulevard<br>Deephaven, MN 55391 |
| **Ask for:** | Funny Poetry pamphlet |

# Super Suspense

Can you solve the mystery? Suspense lovers will go nuts for these short mysteries that you solve yourself. Super Sleuths Amy and Hawkeye get involved in nine different mysteries in this exciting 100-page book.

| Directions: | Write your request on paper, and put it in an envelope. You must enclose **$1.00.** |
|---|---|
| **Write to:** | Meadowbrook Press Department CYSM 18318 Minnetonka Boulevard Deephaven, MN 55391 |
| **Ask for:** | *Loon Lake Monster* mystery book |

# "Soup-er" Writing

If you love writing or drawing pictures, *Stone Soup* is the magazine for you. Every issue contains stories, poems, book reviews, and artwork by kids ages 6 to 13 from all over the world. It's a great way to find out about other kids and to get some creative inspiration.

| Directions: | Write your request on paper (*include your name and address*), and put it in an envelope. You must enclose **$1.50.** (*We think this offer is a good value for the money.*) |
|---|---|
| **Write to:** | Stone Soup P.O. Box 83 Santa Cruz, CA 95063 |
| **Ask for:** | Sample copy of *Stone Soup* magazine |

# Fairy Tales

Do you love the magic of fairy tales like Cinderella and Jack and the Beanstalk? These colorful six-panel cards tell and illustrate your favorite fairy tales. They also fold up into neat little packages that you can send to friends without using envelopes.

| Directions: | Write your request on paper, and put it in an envelope. You must enclose a long self-addressed, stamped envelope and **$1.00** for **each** card you request. |
|---|---|
| Write to: | More Than A Card<br>4334 Earhart Boulevard<br>New Orleans, LA 70125 |
| Ask for: | • Snow White book-card<br>• Hansel and Gretel book-card<br>• Jack and the Beanstalk book-card<br>• Cinderella book-card<br>• Rumpelstilskin book-card<br>• Little Red Riding Hood book-card |

# Nursery Tales

Hey diddle, diddle! These cards feature favorite nursery rhymes and games—share them with a younger brother or sister. You'll find all of the classics in these six-panel illustrated cards.

| Directions: | Write your request on paper, and put it in an envelope. You must enclose a long self-addressed, stamped envelope and **$1.00** for **each** card you request. |
|---|---|
| Write to: | More Than A Card<br>4334 Earhart Boulevard<br>New Orleans, LA 70125 |
| Ask for: | • Lullaby and Goodnight book-card<br>• Mother Goose Rhymes book-card<br>• Car Seat Games book-card |

# Full of Surprises

If you love to do puzzles, mazes, or crosswords, you'll love *SURPRISES*. This exciting magazine is full of educational games and activities, jokes and riddles, arts and crafts ideas, and more.

| **Directions:** | Write your request on paper, and put it in an envelope. You must enclose **$1.00.** |
|---|---|
| **Write to:** | Children's Surprises<br>Samples Department<br>8140 Flying Cloud Drive #202<br>Eden Prairie, MN 55344 |
| **Ask for:** | Sample copy of *SURPRISES* |

# Spark It Up

Looking for something new to do? *SPARK!* magazine will show you how to do all kinds of cool projects like drawing and cartooning, making potato-print T-shirts, carving clay sculptures, making artwork you can eat, and more!

| **Directions:** | Write your request on paper, and put it in an envelope. You must enclose **$1.00.** |
|---|---|
| **Write to:** | *SPARK!*<br>1507 Dana Avenue<br>Cincinnati, OH 45207<br>Attention: Jennifer Jones |
| **Ask for:** | Sample copy of *SPARK!* |

# Young Readers

Explore these exciting magazines by yourself or with a grown-up.

- *Turtle* (ages 2 to 5) is a unique magazine filled with read-to-me stories, hidden pictures, dot-to-dots, coloring pages, and more.

- *Humpty Dumpty's* (ages 4 to 6) entertains and teaches with fun stories, poems, puzzles, and crafts.

- *Children's Playmate* (ages 6 to 8) offers colorfully illustrated stories for beginning readers, intriguing puzzles, games, recipes, cartoons, and activities.

| | |
|---|---|
| **Directions:** | Write your request on paper, and put it in an envelope. You must enclose **$1.00** for **each** magazine you request. |
| **Write to:** | Children's Better Health Institute<br>Department FSK<br>1100 Waterway Boulevard<br>Indianapolis, IN 46202<br>Attention: Chelle |
| **Ask for:** | • *Turtle* magazine<br>• *Humpty Dumpty's* magazine<br>• *Children's Playmate* magazine |

# Older Readers

These three magazines for older readers invite you to learn, laugh, and create.

- *Jack and Jill* (ages 7 to 10) entertains with illustrated fiction, jokes, activities—plus works by kids.
- *Child Life* (ages 9 to 11) offers Diane's Dinosaur comics, Odd Job career profiles, activities, and great stories.
- *Children's Digest* (preteen) features contemporary fiction, articles on important issues, challenging puzzles, book reviews, and cartoons.

| | |
|---|---|
| **Directions:** | Write your request on paper, and put it in an envelope. You must enclose **$1.00** for **each** magazine you request. |
| **Write to:** | Children's Better Health Institute<br>Department FSK<br>1100 Waterway Boulevard<br>Indianapolis, IN 46202<br>Attention: Chelle |
| **Ask for:** | • *Jack and Jill* magazine<br>• *Child Life* magazine<br>• *Children's Digest* magazine |

# Get Informed!

You'll want to read this "Weekly Reader" magazine again and again. It's filled with cool articles about real people, stories, jokes, puzzles, and advice from kids. And each edition has a colorful pull-out poster that you can hang in your room.

| **Directions:** | Write your request on paper, and put it in an envelope. You must enclose **$1.50.** *(We think this offer is a good value for the money.)* |
|---|---|
| **Write to:** | Children's Better Health Institute<br>Department FSK<br>1100 Waterway Boulevard<br>Indianapolis, IN 46202<br>Attention: Chelle |
| **Ask for:** | *U.S. Kids* magazine |

MEADOWBROOK PRESS
1994 EDITION

U.S. MAIL

# SCHOOL SUPPLIES

# Write on

These writing supplies show others that you say no to drugs and alcohol. You'll get two mini notepads and a pencil.

| **Directions:** | Write your request on paper, and put it in an envelope. You must enclose **$1.00.** (*No checks please.*) |
|---|---|
| **Write to:** | Safe Child<br>P.O. Box 40 1594<br>Brooklyn, NY 11240-1594 |
| **Ask for:** | Just Say No notepads and pencil |

# Rule It out

This wiggle ruler will keep you at the head of the class. It's twelve-inches long and says, "Just Say No." You'll also get five anti-drug stickers.

| **Directions:** | Write your request on paper, and put it in an envelope. You must enclose **$1.00.** (*No checks please.*) |
|---|---|
| **Write to:** | Safe Child<br>P.O. Box 40 1594<br>Brooklyn, NY 11240-1594 |
| **Ask for:** | Just Say No wiggle ruler and stickers |

# Out of This World

These mini earth notepads are great for quick notes to friends. And they're small, so you can carry them in your pocket. You'll get two notepads and either a swirly-design or save-the-earth pencil.

| Directions: | Write your request on paper, and put it in an envelope. You must enclose **$1.00.** (*No checks please.*) |
|---|---|
| **Write to:** | Safe Child<br>P.O. Box 40 1594<br>Brooklyn, NY 11240-1594 |
| **Ask for:** | Earth notepads and pencil |

# Over the Rainbow

Your school box isn't complete without a few erasers. These multi-colored erasers are shaped like "love-ly" little hearts. You'll get three.

| Directions: | Write your request on paper, and put it in an envelope. You must enclose a long self-addressed, stamped envelope and **$1.00.** |
|---|---|
| **Write to:** | Mr. Rainbows<br>Department K-64<br>P.O. Box 387<br>Avalon, NJ 08202 |
| **Ask for:** | Three rainbow heart erasers |

# Batter Up!

What kind of baseball bat can you use in class? One that's really a pen! This mini baseball bat pen is autographed by a famous player.

| Directions: | Write your request on paper, and put it in an envelope. You must enclose **$1.00.** |
|---|---|
| **Write to:** | H & B Promotions<br>Department 90 SRC<br>P. O. Box 10<br>Jeffersonville, IN 47130 |
| **Ask for:** | Louisville Slugger® bat pen |

# Wrist Writer

You'll always have handy handwriting with this flexible pen bracelet.

| Directions: | Write your request on paper, and put it in an envelope. You must enclose a long self-addressed, stamped envelope and **$1.00.** |
|---|---|
| **Write to:** | Neetstuf<br>Department N-34<br>P.O. Box 459<br>Stone Harbor, NJ 08247 |
| **Ask for:** | Pen bracelet |

# M-M-Good Memos

Send a "sweet" note to someone special. These memo pads feature delicious treats on every page. You'll get two.

| Directions: | Write your request on paper, and put it in an envelope. You must enclose a long self-addressed, stamped envelope and **$1.00.** |
|---|---|
| Write to: | Mr. Rainbows<br>Department M-24<br>P.O. Box 387<br>Avalon, NJ 08202 |
| Ask for: | "Yummy" memo pads |

# Dig These Dinosaurs

These mini memo pads are great for taking notes in class or writing notes to your friends. Each cover features a different cartoon dinosaur. You'll get three.

| Directions: | Write your request on paper, and put it in an envelope. You must enclose **$1.00.** |
|---|---|
| Write to: | Eleanor Curran<br>Department MM<br>530 Leonard Street<br>Brooklyn, NY 11222 |
| Ask for: | Dinosaur mini memo pads |

# Math in a Flash

How can a ruler help you with math? When it has a multiplication table printed on it! Tilt this mini ruler one way, and you'll see the problems. Tilt it the other way, and you'll see the answers.

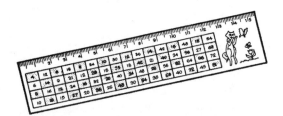

# Oodles of Doodles

Now you can create your own masterpieces with this design ruler. It has movable gears and shapes to help you make unique designs. It can even help you with geometry.

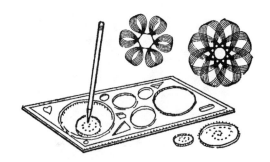

**Directions:** Write your request on paper, and put it in an envelope. You must enclose a long self-addressed, stamped envelope and **$1.00.**

**Write to:**  IPM
Department M-5
P.O. Box 1181
Hammond, IN 46325

**Ask for:**  Just-a-twist ruler

**Directions:** Write your request on paper, and put it in an envelope. You must enclose a long self-addressed, stamped envelope and **$1.00.**

**Write to:**  Mr. Rainbows
Department M-74
P.O. Box 387
Avalon, NJ 08202

**Ask for:**  Design ruler

MEADOWBROOK PRESS
1994
EDITION

U.S.
MAIL

# THE ENVIRONMENT

# Think Green

It's your earth too, so help make it last! Put these environmental awareness stickers on your notebooks, folders, and memo pads to remind yourself not to waste paper—this will save trees and help keep the planet green. You'll get a set of 20 stickers.

IT'S YOUR
EARTH TOO!

Please help
keep it
GREEN!

| Directions: | Write your request on paper, and put it in an envelope. You must enclose a long self-addressed, stamped envelope and **$1.00.** |
|---|---|
| **Write to:** | Fax Marketing<br>Department S<br>460 Carrollton Drive<br>Frederick, MD 21701-6357 |
| **Ask for:** | Environment stickers |

# Save the Earth

Kids like you are doing a lot to save Mother Earth. Join the environmental club that sixth-grader Clinton Hill started, and learn how to make the planet a healthier, happier place for future generations. Send for a Kids for Saving Earth® sticker and club information.

| Directions: | Write your request on paper, and put it in an envelope. You must enclose **$1.00.** |
|---|---|
| **Write to:** | Kids for Saving Earth<br>Department F<br>P.O. Box 47247<br>Plymouth, MN 55447-0247 |
| **Ask for:** | KSE sticker and club information |

# Reduce Litter

Litter is a widespread problem, but you can help make the world a cleaner place. This fact sheet provides information on how to get rid of the litter that pollutes our earth.

| **Directions:** | Write your request on paper, and put it in an envelope. You must enclose a long self-addressed, stamped envelope. |
|---|---|
| **Write to:** | Keep America Beautiful<br>Mill River Plaza<br>9 West Broad Street<br>Stamford, CT 06902 |
| **Ask for:** | Litter Tips fact sheet |

# Ready to Recycle

You can help save the planet. Learn about recycling aluminum, glass, plastic, paper, and more in this coloring and activity book that's printed on recycled paper.

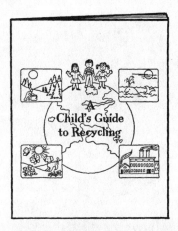

A Child's Guide to Recycling

| **Directions:** | Write your request on paper, and put it in an envelope. You must enclose **$1.00.** |
|---|---|
| **Write to:** | Special Products<br>Department FS<br>P.O. Box 6605<br>Delray Beach, FL 33484 |
| **Ask for:** | Keep Your World Beautiful coloring and activity book |

# Keep It Clean

Show the world that you aren't a litterbug. Wear this "Keep America Beautiful" patch to remind yourself and your friends to protect the environment from all forms of pollution.

| **Directions:** | Write your request on paper, and put it in an envelope. You must enclose a long self-addressed, stamped envelope and **$1.00.** |
|---|---|
| **Write to:** | Keep America Beautiful<br>Mill River Plaza<br>9 West Broad Street<br>Stamford, CT 06902 |
| **Ask for:** | Keep America Beautiful patch |

# Planet Protectors

Help Greenpeace preserve the earth and all the life it supports. These fact sheets will teach you more about the environment and what you can do to make a difference.

| **Directions:** | Write your request on paper, and put it in an envelope. You must enclose a long self-addressed, stamped envelope. |
|---|---|
| **Write to:** | Greenpeace<br>Public Information<br>1436 U Street NW<br>Washington, DC 20009 |
| **Ask for:** | • Atmosphere and Energy fact sheet<br>• Tropical Forests fact sheet<br>• Toxics Prevention fact sheet<br>• Ocean Ecology fact sheet<br>• Nuclear Free Future fact sheet |

## "KIND" of Special

What do endangered animals, recycling, conservation, rock stars, sports figures, and kindness have in common? You'll find them all in *KIND News!* This classroom newspaper shows you how to be kind to animals, people, and the earth.

Kids In Nature's Defense Club

| **Directions:** | Write your request on paper, and put it in an envelope. You must enclose **75¢** for **each** newspaper you request. |
|---|---|
| **Write to:** | KIND News<br>Department FS<br>P.O. Box 362<br>East Haddam, CT 06423-0362 |
| **Ask for:** | • *KIND News Jr.* (grades 2–4)<br>• *KIND News Sr.* (grades 5–6) |

## Take Action!

Ever wonder what you can do to help save the environment? *The HSUS Student Action Guide* has lots of suggestions for forming your own earth and animal protection club. This fun newspaper from the Humane Society of the United States explains how to form a club, hold meetings, target issues, and plan activities.

| **Directions:** | Use a postcard. |
|---|---|
| **Write to:** | HSUS Youth Education Division<br>Department FS<br>P.O. Box 362<br>East Haddam, CT 06423-0362 |
| **Ask for:** | *HSUS Student Action Guide* |

# Let There Be Trees

Trees help convert carbon dioxide in the air into the oxygen that we need to breathe. They also provide valuable shade, shelter, and food for many living things. "Trees for Life" wants to promote awareness of this valuable resource—send for their bumper sticker, button, or free coloring sheet.

| Directions: | Write your request on paper, and put it in an envelope. You must enclose a long self-addressed, stamped envelope for the coloring sheet, **$1.00** for the button, and/or **$1.00** for the bumper sticker. |
|---|---|
| **Write to:** | Trees for Life "Kids" Offer<br>1103 Jefferson<br>Wichita, KS 67203-3559 |
| **Ask for:** | • Coloring sheet<br>• Button<br>• Bumper sticker |

# Get Earth Wise

It's important to conserve water so that crops, trees, animals, people, and other life-forms can live and grow. "Ernie the Earthwise Owl" wants you to learn about water conservation in this coloring and activity book that features tips for saving water.

| Directions: | Write your request on paper, and put it in an envelope. You must enclose **$1.00.** |
|---|---|
| Write to: | Special Products Department FS P.O. Box 6605 Delray Beach, FL 33484 |
| Ask for: | Helping Our Community Save Water coloring book |

# Adopt a Stream

Our streams are in trouble, but you can help. Adopt a stream in your neighborhood, and become a "streamkeeper." These sheets explain how to preserve streams so they stay safe for fish, wildlife, and recreational activities. You'll also get a button with a colorful fish on it.

| Directions: | Write your request on paper, and put it in an envelope. You must enclose a long self-addressed, stamped envelope and **$1.00.** |
|---|---|
| Write to: | Adopt-A-Stream Foundation P.O. Box 5558 Everett, WA 98206 |
| Ask for: | Adopt-A-Stream information sheets and fish button |

# Natural Energy

Learn how the ocean and the earth can be used to create energy. The Conservation and Renewable Energy Inquiry Referral Service (CAREIRS) has two fact sheets to send you about natural energy.

| **Directions:** Use a postcard. | |
| --- | --- |
| **Write to:** | CAREIRS<br>P.O. Box 8900<br>Silver Spring, MD 20907 |
| **Ask for:** | • Ocean Energy—FS 221<br>• Geothermal Energy—FS 188 |

# Land Use

Learn about conservation with these water and soil pamphlets. They'll explain how to prevent flooding and the resulting damage, how grass grows, how to practice soil and water conservation to benefit wildlife, and more!

| **Directions:** Write your request on paper, and put it in an envelope. You must enclose a long self-addressed, stamped envelope for **each** pamphlet you request. | |
| --- | --- |
| **Write to:** | Distribution Section<br>Soil Conservation Service<br>Room 0054-S<br>P.O. Box 2890<br>Washington, DC 20013 |
| **Ask for:** | • Flood Plain Management pamphlet<br>• Grass Makes Its Own Food pamphlet<br>• Going Wild with Soil and Water Conservation booklet<br>• Mulches for Your Garden pamphlet |

MEADOWBROOK PRESS

**1994 EDITION**

U.S. MAIL

# ANIMAL KINGDOM

# For the Birds

Bird-watching is a fun hobby for people of all ages. These pamphlets will tell you what type of feeder and birdseed to buy, how to build or buy your own birdhouse, and how to attract birds to your yard year-round.

| Directions: Use a postcard. | |
|---|---|
| **Write to:** | S. James<br>Consumer Information Center<br>Pueblo, CO 81009 |
| **Ask for:** | • Backyard Bird Feeding pamphlet—580Z<br>• Homes for Birds pamphlet—582Z<br>• Attract Birds pamphlet—579Z |

# Pampered Pets

A pet is a member of your family, so it's important to give it proper care. This pamphlet tells you what a veterinary exam is all about. You'll also get a sticker with a cat, dog, and bird on it to show that you're a kid who cares about pets.

| Directions: | Write your request on paper, and put it in an envelope. You must enclose a long self-addressed, stamped envelope. |
|---|---|
| **Write to:** | American Animal Hospital Association<br>P.O. Box 150899<br>Denver, CO 80215-0899<br>Attention: MSC |
| **Ask for:** | Health Exams pamphlet and Caring Kids sticker |

# Kitten Care

When your kitten purrs it usually means it's happy. Kittens need lots of love and care. Learn more about new-kitten care in these three pamphlets and fun coloring book.

YOU AND YOUR KITTEN

| Directions: | Write your request on paper, and put it in an envelope. You must enclose a long self-addressed, stamped envelope for **each** pamphlet you request. The coloring book is free—use a postcard. |
|---|---|
| Write to: | ALPO Pet Center P.O. Box 25200-F Lehigh Valley, PA 18002-5200 |
| Ask for: | • A Medical Passport for a Healthy Cat pamphlet<br>• Doctor, You Won't Believe What My Cat Just Did pamphlet<br>• Pets on the Go pamphlet<br>• You and Your Kitten coloring book |

# Meow Meow

Are you a cat lover? Then you'll love this "purrfectly" wonderful bumper sticker from the Cat Fanciers' Association. It features helpful information on cat care.

The Cat Fanciers' Association, Inc. **Help Your Cat Live Longer**
• *Keep Your Cat Indoors*
• *Neuter & Spay Your Pet*
*It's the Humane Way!*

| Directions: | Write your request on paper, and put it in an envelope. You must enclose a long self-addressed, stamped envelope and **50¢.** |
|---|---|
| Write to: | Bumper Sticker The Cat Fanciers' Association 918 Millard Court West Daytona Beach, FL 32117-4217 |
| Ask for: | Bumper sticker |

# Puppy Love

It's important to take good care of your new puppy or dog so it stays healthy and happy. Learn about proper canine care in these three pamphlets and fun coloring book.

You and your puppy

| **Directions:** | Write your request on paper, and put it in an envelope. You must enclose a long self-addressed, stamped envelope for **each** pamphlet you request. The coloring book is free—use a postcard. |
|---|---|
| **Write to:** | ALPO Pet Center<br>P.O. Box 25200-F<br>Lehigh Valley, PA 18002-5200 |
| **Ask for:** | • Your Courteous Canine pamphlet<br>• Puppy Proof Your Home pamphlet<br>• Puppies, Parents, and Kids pamphlet<br>• You and Your Puppy coloring book |

# Roving Rover

Is your family moving? Moving to a new home will mean lots of changes for you and your dog. This bookmark gives helpful tips on how to make the move pleasant for your pooch.

| **Directions:** | Write your request on paper, and put it in an envelope. You must enclose a long self-addressed, stamped envelope. |
|---|---|
| **Write to:** | The American Kennel Club<br>Public Education<br>51 Madison Avenue<br>New York, NY 10010 |
| **Ask for:** | Dogs on the Move bookmark |

# Horsing Around

In the old days, families drove to church or across the country in carriages drawn by harness horses. Today these Standardbreds are used for the sport of harness racing. If you're into horses, send for this fun coloring book.

| Directions: | Use a postcard. |
| --- | --- |
| **Write to:** | U.S. Trotting Association Publicity Department 750 Michigan Avenue Columbus, OH 43215-1191 |
| **Ask for:** | The Story of Harness Racing coloring book |

# Horse Sense

The high-stepping Saddlebreds, known for their grace and personality, gained fame during the Civil War when they served as mounts for famous generals like Lee and Grant. This offer includes a coloring poster, logo sticker, and informative brochures.

| Directions: | Write your request on paper, and put it in an envelope. You must enclose **$1.00.** |
| --- | --- |
| **Write to:** | ASHA 4093 Iron Works Pike Lexington, KY 40511 Attention: Youth Coordinator |
| **Ask for:** | Coloring poster, sticker, and brochures |

# A Horse, of Course

If you're crazy about horses, you'll love this offer: a colorful poster to hang in your bedroom, a matching postcard to send to a friend, and a booklet. You'll learn about America's oldest horse breed and the exciting youth programs available to horse enthusiasts ages 7 to 19.

| Directions: | Write your request on paper, and put it in an envelope. You must enclose **$1.00.** |
|---|---|
| **Write to:** | AQHA<br>Department FS<br>1600 Quarter Horse Drive<br>Amarillo, TX 79104 |
| **Ask for:** | American Quarter Horse poster, postcard, and booklet |

# Awesome Arabians

The versatile Arabian horse can do it all—halter, western, hunter, English, trail, dressage, and jumping! The International Arabian Horse Association has lots of information about this beautiful breed of horse. You can also get a large wall chart featuring all the parts of the horse.

| Directions: | Write your request on paper, and put it in an envelope. You must enclose **$1.00** if you request the wall chart. |
|---|---|
| **Write to:** | IAHA<br>Department Y<br>P.O. Box 33696<br>Denver, CO 80233-0696 |
| **Ask for:** | • General Information packet<br>• Parts of the Horse wall chart |

# AMERICAN HISTORY AND GEOGRAPHY

# Pledge Allegiance

Show your patriotism! You can sew this American flag patch to your jean jacket, baseball cap, or backpack.

| **Directions:** | Write your request on paper, and put it in an envelope. You must enclose a long self-addressed, stamped envelope and **50¢.** |
|---|---|
| **Write to:** | Pineapple Appeal<br>Box 197<br>Owatonna, MN 55060 |
| **Ask for:** | American flag patch |

# Wave It Proudly

Here's a mini replica of the American flag on a pole. Be sure to display it on Flag Day (June 14).

| **Directions:** | Write your request on paper, and put it in an envelope. You must enclose a long self-addressed, stamped envelope and **50¢.** |
|---|---|
| **Write to:** | Parker Flags & Pennants<br>5746 Plunkett Street, Suite 4<br>Hollywood, FL 33023-2346 |
| **Ask for:** | U.S. Flag |

# Stars and Stripes

Tradition says that Betsy Ross designed the original American flag in 1776. But some sources disagree. Read all about Betsy Ross and other flag stories in this seven-page booklet from the Veterans of Foreign Wars of the U.S.

| **Directions:** | Write your request on paper, and put it in an envelope. You must enclose a long self-addressed, stamped envelope. |
|---|---|
| **Write to:** | VFW National Headquarters<br>Americanism Department<br>406 West 34th Street<br>Kansas City, MO 64111 |
| **Ask for:** | Ten Short Flag Stories booklet |

# Star-Spangled Banner

The Battle of Baltimore, during the War of 1812, was more than just an American victory—it sparked Francis Scott Key's writing of *The Star-Spangled Banner,* our national anthem. Send for these reading materials about the American flag and Fort McHenry to learn more. You'll also get a copy of the original *Star-Spangled Banner* song.

| **Directions:** | Write your request on paper, and put it in an envelope. You must enclose $1.00. |
|---|---|
| **Write to:** | The Star-Spangled Banner Flag House<br>Corner of Albemarle Street<br>844 East Pratt Street<br>Baltimore, MD 21202 |
| **Ask for:** | Flag House materials for kids |

# Father of Our Country

Did you know that George Washington never chopped down a cherry tree or wore a wig? Learn some facts about his life and presidency in a collection of brochures, booklets, and post-cards. You'll also get excerpts from his boyhood journal, a brief biography, and a "scratch and learn" quiz card.

| Directions: | Write your request on paper, and put it in an envelope. You must enclose **$1.00.** |
|---|---|
| **Write to:** | Mount Vernon Ladies' Association Education Department Mount Vernon, VA 22121 |
| **Ask for:** | George Washington materials for kids |

# A Trace of the Past

Mount Rushmore, the Washington Memorial, and the Statue of Liberty are some historic symbols in the United States. Now you can create your own historic scenes with this set of patriotic tracing shapes.

| Directions: | Write your request on paper, and put it in an envelope. You must enclose **$1.00.** |
|---|---|
| **Write to:** | Lightning Enterprises P.O. Box 16121 West Palm Beach, FL 33416 |
| **Ask for:** | Patriotic tracing shapes |

# Historic Gettysburg

Gettysburg, Pennsylvania, was the site of the most famous Civil War battle. Today the town remembers and honors that battle with more than 1,000 monuments and other attractions. This 64-page guide tells you all about the history of Gettysburg.

| Directions: | Use a postcard. |
| --- | --- |
| **Write to:** | Gettysburg Travel Council<br>Department 401<br>35 Carlisle Street<br>Gettysburg, PA 17325 |
| **Ask for:** | Gettysburg tourism booklet |

# History of Paper

Trace the history of paper in the United States using this large poster. You can also get some materials with information about paper's environmental impact, paper recycling, and instructions for how to make your own paper. Specify which items you want.

| Directions: | Use a postcard. |
| --- | --- |
| **Write to:** | American Forest & Paper Association<br>1111 19th Street, NW<br>Washington, DC 20036 |
| **Ask for:** | • How Paper Came to America poster<br>• Paper and Paper Manufacture booklet<br>• How You Can Make Paper foldout |

# Fun on the Run

Use this fun booklet when you travel across the U.S.A. It has 31 pages and is filled with great games the whole family can play while traveling by car.

| **Directions:** | Write your request on paper, and put it in an envelope. You must enclose **$1.50.** (*We think this offer is a good value for the money.*) |
|---|---|
| **Write to:** | The Beavers<br>Department FS<br>HCR 70, Box 537<br>Laporte, MN 56461 |
| **Ask for:** | Travel Games booklet |

# Family on the Go

Car trips with your family are lots of fun—especially when you play travel games together! Send for this license plate game that features a U.S. map and a geography quiz. You'll also get a family travel guides catalog to make your next vacation extra special.

| **Directions:** | Write your request on paper, and put it in an envelope. You must enclose **$1.00.** |
|---|---|
| **Write to:** | Carousel Press<br>Family Travel Guides Game<br>P.O. Box 6061<br>Albany, CA 94706-0061 |
| **Ask for:** | U.S. License Plate Game and catalog |

# U.S.A. Magnets

Now you can have a magnet with your home state stamp on it. Collect all 50 plus the District of Columbia for a full set.

| Directions: | Write your request on paper, and put it in an envelope. You must enclose **75¢** for **each** magnet you request. |
|---|---|
| Write to: | Hicks Specialties<br>1308 68th Lane North<br>Brooklyn Center, MN 55430 |
| Ask for: | State stamp magnet (*specify the state you want*) |

# Take a Hike

Now you can have a colorful map of the United States that shows our 156 National Forests. Wherever you are, you're probably no more than a day's drive from a National Forest where you and your family can hike, fish, camp, or just sit back and enjoy the sights.

| Directions: | Write your request on paper, and put it in an envelope. You must enclose **$1.00.** |
|---|---|
| Write to: | Consumer Information Center<br>Department 133Z<br>Pueblo, CO 81009 |
| Ask for: | A Guide to Your National Forests pamphlet/map |

# Be a Pen Pal

Make a friend in another part of the country without even leaving your house! A pen pal is a special friend you write letters to—you can exchange information about your state, neighborhood, school, and family with another kid your age who shares similar interests. The Dolphin Pen Pal Center will provide you with your new pen pal's address so you can start writing.

| **Directions:** | Write your request on paper (*and include your age, grade, and favorite activities*), and put it in an envelope. You must enclose a long self-addressed, stamped envelope and **$1.00.** |
|---|---|
| **Write to:** | Dolphin Pen Pal Center<br>Department FSFK<br>32-B Shelter Cove Lane<br>Hilton Head Island, SC 29928 |
| **Ask for:** | U.S. pen pal |

# Prairie Days

Do you know who was called "Halfpint" on the television show "Little House on the Prairie"? Send for this Laura Ingalls Wilder and Rose Wilder Lane timeline to learn more about the history of the real Ingalls family.

| **Directions:** | Write your request on paper, and put it in an envelope. You must enclose a long self-addressed, stamped envelope and **$1.00.** |
|---|---|
| **Write to:** | Bluestocking Press<br>Department FSK<br>P.O. Box 1014<br>Placerville, CA 95667 |
| **Ask for:** | Laura Ingalls Wilder timeline |

# America's Sites

The United States has a wealth of history and natural beauty. Now you can explore America's sites, parks, and monuments with these informative publications.

| | |
|---|---|
| **Directions:** | Use a postcard. |
| **Write to:** | The tourism offices listed here |
| **Ask for:** | Tourism information |

**Booker T. Washington**
Booker T. Washington National Monument
Route 3, Box 310
Hardy, VA 24101

**Carlsbad Caverns**
Carlsbad Caverns National Park
3225 National Parks Highway
Carlsbad, NM 88220

**Custer's Last Stand**
Little Big Horn National Monument
P.O. Box 39
Crow Agency, MT 59022

**Death Valley**
Death Valley National Monument
Death Valley, CA 92328

**Dinosaurs**
Dinosaur National Monument
P.O. Box 210
Dinosaur, CO 81610

**Edison National Historic Site**
Main Street and Lakeside Avenue
West Orange, NJ 07052

**Frederick Douglass National Historic Site**
1411 W Street SE
Washington, DC 20020

**Fort Sumter**
Fort Sumter National Monument
1214 Middle Street
Sullivan's Island, SC 29482

**Grand Teton**
Grand Teton National Park
P.O. Drawer 170
Moose, WY 83012

**Ice Age**
Ice Age Trail Project
700 Ray-O-Vac Drive, Suite 100
Madison, WI 53711

**Lewis and Clark**
Lewis and Clark National Historic Trail
700 Ray-O-Vac Drive, Suite 100
Madison, WI 53711

**Lincoln Memorial**
c/o National Park Service
NCP-Central
900 Ohio Drive, SW
Washington, DC 20242

**Martin Luther King, Jr. National Historic Site**
526 Auburn Avenue NE
Atlanta, GA 30312

**Montezuma Castle**
Montezuma Castle National Monument
P.O. Box 219
Camp Verde, AZ 86322

**Monticello**
Virginia State Chamber of Commerce
9 South Fifth Street
Richmond, VA 23219

**Mount Rushmore**
Mount Rushmore National Memorial
P.O. Box 268
Keystone, SD 57751-0268

**Mount Vernon**
Virginia State Chamber of Commerce
9 South Fifth Street
Richmond, VA 23219

**National Cowboy Hall of Fame**
1700 Northeast 63rd Street
Oklahoma City, OK 73111

**Nez Perce**
Nez Perce National Historical Park
P.O. Box 93
Spalding, ID 83551

**North Country**
North Country
700 Ray-O-Vac Drive, Suite 100
Madison, WI 53711

**San Antonio**
San Antonio Missions
National Historical Park
2202 Roosevelt Avenue
San Antonio, TX 78210-4919

**Sunset Crater/Wupatki National Monuments**
Route 3, Box 149
Flagstaff, AZ 86004

**Thomas Jefferson Memorial**
c/o National Park Service
NCP-Central
900 Ohio Drive, SW
Washington, DC 20242

**Valley Forge**
Valley Forge Convention and Visitors Bureau
P.O. Box 331
Norristown, PA 19404

**Vietnam Veterans Memorial**
c/o National Park Service
NCP-Central
900 Ohio Drive, SW
Washington, DC 20242

**Washington Monument**
c/o National Park Service
NCP-Central
900 Ohio Drive, SW
Washington, DC 20242

**White House**
National Capital Region
National Park Service
President's Park
1100 Ohio Drive, SW
Washington, DC 20242

**Williamsburg**
Director of Media Relations
Colonial Williamsburg Foundation
P.O. Box 1776
Williamsburg, VA 23187

**Wisconsin Dells Visitor and Convention Bureau**
701 Superior Street
Wisconsin Dells, WI 53965

# Discover America

Whether you're planning a family trip or are just curious about your country, you'll want to send for these state and city tourism packets. Every state listed here will send something special.

| | |
|---|---|
| **Directions:** | Use a postcard. |
| **Write to:** | The state offices listed here |
| **Ask for:** | Tourism information |

## Alabama
Alabama Bureau of Tourism & Travel
401 Adams Avenue
Montgomery, AL 36104

Greater Birmingham Convention & Visitors Center
2200 Ninth Avenue North
Birmingham, AL 35203

## Alaska
Alaska Division of Tourism
P.O. Box 110801
Juneau, AK 99811-0801

Anchorage Convention & Visitors Bureau
1600 A Street, Suite 200
Anchorage, AK 99501

## Arizona
Arizona Office of Tourism
1100 West Washington
Phoenix, AZ 85007

Phoenix and Valley of the Sun Convention & Visitors Bureau
1 Arizona Plaza
400 East Van Buren, Suite 600
Phoenix, AZ 85004-2290

## Arkansas
Tourism Division
Arkansas Department of Parks & Tourism
One Capitol Mall
Little Rock, AR 72201

Greater Little Rock Chamber of Commerce
One Spring Building
Little Rock, AR 72201

## California
California Office of Tourism
801 K Street, Suite 1600
Sacramento, CA 95814

Los Angeles Convention & Visitors Bureau
633 West Fifth Street, Suite 6000
Los Angeles, CA 90071

San Diego Convention & Visitors Bureau
1200 Third Avenue, Suite 824
San Diego, CA 92101

**Colorado**
Colorado Tourism Board
1625 Broadway, Suite 1700
Denver, CO 80202

**Connecticut**
Department of Economic Development
Tourism Division
865 Brook Street
Rocky Hill, CT 06067-3405

**Delaware**
Delaware Development Office
99 Kings Highway
P.O. Box 1401
Dover, DE 19903

**District of Columbia**
Washington Convention & Visitors Association
1212 New York Avenue NW, 6th Floor
Washington, DC 20005

**Florida**
Florida Division of Tourism Services
Bureau of Visitor Services
107 West Gaines Street, Room 501D
Tallahassee, FL 32399-2000

Jacksonville Convention & Visitors Bureau
3 Independent Drive
Jacksonville, FL 32202

Greater Miami Convention & Visitors Bureau
701 Brickell Avenue, Suite 2700
Miami, FL 33131

**Georgia**
Atlanta Convention & Visitors Bureau
233 Peachtree Street, Suite 2000
Atlanta, GA 30303

Georgia Department of Industry & Trade
Tourist Division
P.O. Box 1776
Atlanta, GA 30301

**Hawaii**
Hawaii Visitors Bureau
2270 Kalakaua Avenue
Honolulu, HI 96815

**Idaho**
Idaho Department of Commerce
State House Mail
700 West State Street
Boise, ID 83720-2700

**Illinois**
Department of Commerce & Community Affairs
Information and Distribution Center
620 East Adams Street, Floor M1
Springfield, IL 62701

Illinois Tourist Information Center
100 West Randolph Street, Suite 3-400
Chicago, IL 60601

**Indiana**
Tourism Development
Department of Commerce
1 North Capitol, Suite 700
Indianapolis, IN 46204

**Iowa**
Division of Tourism
200 East Grand
Des Moines, IA 50309

**Kansas**
Kansas Travel & Tourism Information
Department of Commerce
700 SW Harrison, Suite 1300
Topeka, KS 66603

**Kentucky**
Tourism Cabinet
Capitol Plaza Tower
500 Mero Street, Suite 22
Frankfort, KY 40601

Convention & Visitors Bureau
400 South First Street
Louisville, KY 40202

**Louisiana**
Louisiana Office of Tourism
Inquiries Station
P.O. Box 94291
Baton Rouge, LA 70804-9291

Greater New Orleans Tourism & Convention
Commission
1520 Sugar Bowl Drive
New Orleans, LA 70112

**Maine**
Department of Economic & Community
Development
Office of Tourism
193 State Street
Augusta, ME 04333

**Maryland**
Office of Tourism
Visitors Center
23 West Chesapeake
Towson, MD 21204

Baltimore Area and Information Center
300 West Pratt Street
Baltimore, MD 21201

**Massachusetts**
Massachusetts Travel & Tourism
100 Cambridge Street, 13th Floor
Boston, MA 02202

Greater Boston Convention & Visitors Bureau
Prudential Tower
P.O. Box 490, Suite 400
Boston, MA 02199

**Michigan**
Michigan Travel Bureau
P.O. Box 30226
Lansing, MI 48909

Metropolitan Detroit Convention &
Visitors Bureau
100 Renaissance Center, Suite 1950
Detroit, MI 48243-1056

Flint Convention & Visitors Bureau
Northbank Center, Suite 101-A
400 North Saginaw
Flint, MI 48502

**Minnesota**
Minnesota Office of Tourism
100 Metro Square Building
121 Seventh Place East
St. Paul, MN 55101

Greater Minneapolis Convention &
Visitors Association
1219 Marquette Avenue South, Suite 300
Minneapolis, MN 55403

St. Paul Convention & Visitors Bureau
101 Norwest Center
55 East Fifth Street
St. Paul, MN 55101-1713

**Mississippi**
Mississippi Division of Tourism
P.O. Box 849
Jackson, MS 39205-0849

Natchez Convention & Visitors Commission
P.O. Box 1485
Natchez, MS 39121

**Missouri**
Convention & Visitors Bureau of Greater
Kansas City
City Center Square
1100 Main, Suite 2550
Kansas City, MO 64105

Convention & Visitors Bureau of Greater St. Louis
10 South Broadway, Suite 1000
St. Louis, MO 63102

**Montana**
Montana Department of Commerce
Travel Promotion
1424 Ninth Avenue
Helena, MT 59620

**Nebraska**
Nebraska Department of Economic Development
Travel & Tourism Division
301 Centennial Mall South
P.O. Box 94666
Lincoln, NE 68509

**Nevada**
Nevada Commission of Tourism
5151 South Carson Street
Carson City, NV 89710

Las Vegas Convention & Visitors Authority
3150 South Paradise Road
Las Vegas, NV 89109

**New Jersey**
New Jersey Division of Tourism
P.O. Box CN 826
Trenton, NJ 08625

Atlantic City Convention & Visitors Bureau
2301 Boardwalk
Atlantic City, NJ 08401

**New Mexico**
New Mexico Department of Tourism
Lamy Building
491 Old Santa Fe Trail
Santa Fe, NM 87503

**New York**
New York State Department of Economics
Division of Tourism
1515 Broadway, 51st Floor
New York, NY 10036

New York Convention & Visitors Bureau
Two Columbus Circle
New York, NY 10019

**North Carolina**
North Carolina Department of Commerce
Travel & Tourism Division
430 North Salisbury Street
Raleigh, NC 27603

Charlotte Convention & Visitors Bureau
122 East Stonewall Street
Charlotte, NC 28202

**North Dakota**
North Dakota Travel Department
Liberty Memorial Building
604 East Boulevard
Bismarck, ND 58505

**Ohio**
Ohio Office of Travel & Tourism
77 South High Street, 29th Floor
Columbus, OH 43266

Greater Cincinnati Convention & Visitors Bureau
300 West Sixth Street
Cincinnati, OH 45202

**Oklahoma**
Oklahoma Tourism & Recreation Department
2401 North Lincoln Boulevard, Suite 500
Oklahoma City, OK 73105-4492

**Oregon**
Oregon Tourism Division
775 Summer Street NE
Salem, OR 97310

Portland/Oregon Visitors Association
26 SW Salmon Street
Portland, OR 97204-3299

**Pennsylvania**
Pennsylvania Department of Commerce
Bureau of Travel Development
453 Forum Building
Harrisburg, PA 17120

Philadelphia Convention & Visitors Bureau
1515 Market Street, Suite 2020
Philadelphia, PA 19102

Greater Pittsburgh Convention & Visitors Bureau
4 Gateway Center, Suite 514
Pittsburgh, PA 15222

**Rhode Island**
Rhode Island Department of Economic
Development
Tourist Promotion Division
Seven Jackson Walkway
Providence, RI 02903

**South Carolina**
South Carolina Department of Parks, Recreation,
& Tourism
Division of Tourism
1205 Pendleton Street
Columbia, SC 29201

**South Dakota**
South Dakota Department of Tourism
711 East Wells Avenue
Pierre, SD 57501-3369

**Tennessee**
Tennessee Tourist Development
P.O. Box 23170
Nashville, TN 37202

Knoxville Convention & Visitors Bureau
P.O. Box 15012
Knoxville, TN 37901

Memphis Convention & Visitors Bureau
45 Union Avenue
Memphis, TN 38103

**Texas**
Texas Department of Commerce
Tourism Division
P.O. Box 12728
Austin, TX 78711

Dallas Convention & Visitors Bureau
1201 Elm Street, Suite 2000
Dallas, TX 75270

Fort Worth Convention & Visitors Bureau
415 Throckmorton Street
Fort Worth, TX 76102

**Utah**
Utah Travel Council
Council Hall, Capitol Hill
Salt Lake City, UT 84114

Salt Lake Convention & Visitors Bureau
180 South West Temple
Salt Lake City, UT 84101-1493

**Vermont**
Vermont Travel Division
134 State Street
Montpelier, VT 05602

**Virginia**
Virginia Division of Tourism
1021 East Cary
Richmond, VA 23219

Norfolk Convention & Visitors Bureau
236 East Plume Street
Norfolk, VA 23510

**Washington**
Department of Trade & Economic Development
Tourism Development Division
P.O. Box 42500
Olympia, WA 98504-2500

Seattle-King County Convention & Visitors Bureau
520 Pike Street, Suite 1300
Seattle, WA 98101

**West Virginia**
West Virginia Division of Tourism and Parks
1900 Kanawha Boulevard
Building 6, Room B564
Charleston, WV 25305-0317

**Wisconsin**
Wisconsin Tourism
P.O. Box 7970
Madison, WI 53707

Greater Milwaukee Convention & Visitors Bureau
510 West Kilbourn
Milwaukee, WI 53203

**Wyoming**
Wyoming Travel Commission
I-25 at College Drive
Cheyenne, WY 82002

Casper Area Chamber of Commerce
P.O. Box 399
500 North Center
Casper, WY 82601

# ACTIVITIES

# Neat Ideas!

Make cool toys out of things that you have around the house with these idea sheets.

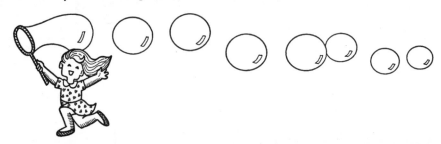

| **Directions:** | Write your request on paper, and put it in an envelope. You must enclose **50¢** for **each** sheet you request. |
|---|---|
| **Write to:** | Children's Museum Shop<br>300 Congress Street<br>Boston, MA 02210<br>Attention: Idea Sheets |
| **Ask for:** | • Balloon and Funnel Pump idea sheet (enclose **50¢**)<br>• Tin Can Pump idea sheet (enclose **50¢**)<br>• Making Large Bubbles idea sheet (enclose **50¢**)<br>• Special Bubble Machine idea sheet (enclose **50¢**)<br>• Pie Plate Water Wheel idea sheet (enclose **50¢**)<br>• Raceways: Experiments with Marbles and Tracks idea sheet (enclose **50¢**)<br>• Spinning Top That Writes idea sheet (enclose **50¢**)<br>• Building Blocks from Milk Cartons idea sheet (enclose **50¢**)<br>• Siphon Bottles idea sheet (enclose **50¢**)<br>• Explorations with Food Coloring idea sheet (enclose **50¢**)<br>• Stained Glass Cookies idea sheet (enclose **50¢**)<br>• Making Simple Books idea sheet (enclose **50¢**)<br>• Organdy Screening idea sheet (enclose **50¢**) |

# Puppet Play

Do you like to put on puppet shows for your friends and family? This kit contains everything you need to make three pull-string puppets, plus materials for different hats and facial expressions.

| **Directions:** | Write your request on paper, and put it in an envelope. You must enclose **$1.00.** |
|---|---|
| **Write to:** | Alaska Craft<br>Department PS<br>Box 11-1102<br>Anchorage, AK 99511-1102 |
| **Ask for:** | Pull-string paper puppets |

# "Play Clay" Day

Gloomy outside? It might be a "Play Clay" day! Have lots of fun with clay you make with baking soda and other common ingredients. This fold-out shows you how to make jewelry, ornaments, and more!

| **Directions:** | Write your request on paper, and put it in an envelope. You must enclose a long self-addressed, stamped envelope. |
|---|---|
| **Write to:** | Play Clay<br>Church & Dwight<br>Arm & Hammer Division<br>P. O. Box 7648-FS94<br>Princeton, NJ 08543-7648 |
| **Ask for:** | How to Make Play Clay activity foldout |

# Get in the Action

An accurate throw is better than a strong one in baseball. Learn more about strategies of the game in this baseball playmaking guide. You'll also get a baseball postcard and pencil.

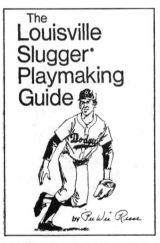

| Directions: | Write your request on paper, and put it in an envelope. You must enclose **$1.00.** |
|---|---|
| Write to: | Pony Baseball<br>P.O. Box 225<br>Washington, PA 15301 |
| Ask for: | Pony Baseball guide, postcard, and pencil |

# Watch Them Grow

Do you have a green thumb? Then try gardening! You and the sun can turn these seed packets, filled with hundreds of carrot and lettuce seeds, into a healthy salad.

| Directions: | Write your request on paper, and put it in an envelope. You must enclose **$1.00.** |
|---|---|
| Write to: | Butterbrooke Farm<br>78-K Barry Road<br>Oxford, CT 06478-1529 |
| Ask for: | Special kids' salad garden seeds |

# Mini Mouse

Now you can have a mouse in your house. This craft kit contains all you need to create a cute and furry finger-puppet mouse. You'll get a set of mouse-making materials and an instruction sheet.

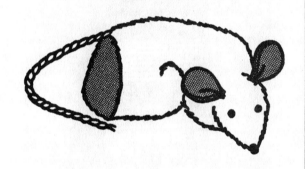

| **Directions:** | Write your request on paper, and put it in an envelope. You must enclose **$1.00.** |
|---|---|
| **Write to:** | The Woolie Works—Mouse<br>6201 East Huffman Road<br>Anchorage, AK 99516-2440 |
| **Ask for:** | Finger Mouse craft kit |

# Roller Kids

This coloring and activity book features the fun-loving "Roller Kids." It has pages to color, word games, and other fun activities.

| **Directions:** | Write your request on paper, and put it in an envelope. You must enclose **$1.00.** |
|---|---|
| **Write to:** | Roller Skating Associations<br>7301 Georgetown Road<br>Suite 123<br>Indianapolis, IN 46268 |
| **Ask for:** | Roller Kids coloring and activity book |

# Count Your Stitches

This simple counted cross-stitch kit is perfect for beginners. It includes all the materials you need to make a bookmark that features a dinosaur and says "Read," plus a simple instruction sheet. When you've completed your bookmark, take it to school to show your teacher or librarian.

| | |
|---|---|
| **Directions:** | Write your request on paper, and put it in an envelope. You must enclose a long self-addressed, stamped envelope and **$1.00**. |
| **Write to:** | Andy's Dandies<br>c/o Adrienne Asnin<br>76 West Eckerson Road<br>Spring Valley, NY 10977 |
| **Ask for:** | Dinosaur bookmark kit |

# Make It Yourself

Here's a simple cross-stitch kit that's really cool—it's a popsicle. You'll get all the materials you need to make a colorful popsicle magnet, plus a simple instruction sheet. When you've completed your magnet, stick it on your refrigerator or freezer.

| | |
|---|---|
| **Directions:** | Write your request on paper, and put it in an envelope. You must enclose a long self-addressed, stamped envelope and **$1.00**. |
| **Write to:** | Andy's Dandies #2<br>c/o Adrienne Asnin<br>76 West Eckerson Road<br>Spring Valley, NY 10977 |
| **Ask for:** | Popsicle magnet kit |

# Beautiful Bangles

This glittery bracelet is almost as fun to make as it is to wear. You'll get all the supplies to make one bracelet, plus an instruction sheet.

| **Directions:** | Write your request on paper, and put it in an envelope. You must enclose a long self-addressed, stamped envelope and **$1.00**. |
|---|---|
| **Write to:** | Grin 'n' Barrett Department T 5701 North Magnolia Avenue Rialto, CA 92377 |
| **Ask for:** | Glittery Toobs bracelet kit |

# Cool Cats

Add a little fun to your clothes with these **cool** cats. Get a grown-up to help you iron **on** these velour transfers, and you'll have five **crazy cats** dancing across your shirt, pants, or jean jacket!

| **Directions:** | Write your request on paper, and put it in an envelope. You must enclose a long self-addressed, stamped envelope and **$1.00**. |
|---|---|
| **Write to:** | Pineapple Appeal Department FS P.O. Box 197 Owatonna, MN 55060 |
| **Ask for:** | Cat iron on transfers |

# Checkmate

Chess has a long, rich history. Most historians believe it was invented about 1,300 years ago in India. Today the game continues to fascinate anyone who enjoys a challenge. Send for this sixteen-page booklet on winning strategies and this pamphlet on getting involved in the world of chess.

| Directions: | Write your request on paper, and put it in an envelope. You must enclose a long self-addressed, stamped envelope for **each** item you request. |
|---|---|
| **Write to:** | Barbara A. DeMaro<br>U.S. Chess Federation<br>186 Route 9W<br>New Windsor, NY 12553 |
| **Ask for:** | • Ten Tips to Winning Chess booklet<br>• Get Moving! pamphlet |

# Scratch and Win

"Dr. Scratchov"™ has created some awesome scratch-off games featuring comic book-like art and some really creepy characters! Each game pack contains three scratch-off games so you and a friend can play the best two out of three. Collect the games, and earn enough points for fun free items like a yo-yo, bike siren, or even a skateboard!

| Directions: | Write your request on paper, and put it in an envelope. You must enclose **$1.00.** |
|---|---|
| **Write to:** | Decipher<br>Department FSK<br>253 Granby Street<br>Norfolk, VA 23501-0056 |
| **Ask for:** | Scratchees™ game pack |

MEADOWBROOK PRESS
1994 EDITION

U.S. MAIL

# SAFETY AND HEALTH

# Plan Ahead

SADD (Students Against Driving Drunk) is an organization that works to end death and injury on the highways due to drinking and driving. This pamphlet contains a "Contract for Life" for you and your parents to discuss and sign. You can also share it with an older brother or sister who already drives. You'll get a pamphlet and a SADD bumper sticker.

| Directions: | Write your request on paper, and put it in an envelope. You must enclose a long self-addressed, stamped envelope with **two 29¢** stamps and **$1.00.** |
|---|---|
| **Write to:** | SADD<br>P.O. Box 800<br>Marlboro, MA 01752 |
| **Ask for:** | Bob Anastas Speaks to Parents pamphlet and SADD bumper sticker |

# Safety First

"SAFE KIDS are no accident!"® is the motto of the National SAFE KIDS Campaign. To be a safe kid, you need to stay away from danger and take precautions every day. These magazines are filled with fun games, experiments, songs, and activities that teach you to play it safe.

| **Directions:** | Write your request on paper, and put it in an envelope. You must enclose **$1.00** for **each** item you request. |
| --- | --- |
| **Write to:** | National SAFE KIDS Campaign<br>111 Michigan Avenue, NW<br>Washington, DC 20010-2970 |
| **Ask for:** | • Traffic safety magazine for kids<br>• Fire safety magazine for kids |

# Carry Your I.D.

Staying safe is important. This "child file" is a good way to keep a record of all your physical characteristics for easy identification, just in case you get hurt or lost. The file contains a place for your photo, helpful safety tips, and a fingerprint kit.

| **Directions:** | Write your request on paper, and put it in an envelope. You must enclose a long self-addressed, stamped envelope and **$1.00.** |
| --- | --- |
| **Write to:** | Special Products<br>Department FS<br>34 Romeyn Avenue<br>Amsterdam, NY 12010 |
| **Ask for:** | ChildFile |

# Play It Safe

Now you can learn how to take good care of your bicycle and how to ride it safely. Pick up these and other safety and health habits from this pamphlet and coloring book.

| Directions: | Write your request on paper, and put it in an envelope. You must enclose a long self-addressed, stamped envelope for the pamphlet. The coloring book is free—use a postcard. |
|---|---|
| Write to: | Aetna Life & Casualty<br>Public Service Library RE6H<br>151 Farmington Avenue<br>Hartford, CT 06156 |
| Ask for: | · Safe Biking pamphlet<br>· Play It Safe coloring book |

# Be a Safe Biker

This coloring book teaches you about bike safety and why these measures are important. You'll learn everything from hand signals to how to check your bike for safety before you ride.

| Directions: | Use a postcard. |
|---|---|
| Write to: | Sandoz<br>59 Route 10<br>East Hanover, NJ 07936<br>Attention: Mature Market |
| Ask for: | Helping with Bike Safety coloring book |

# Use Your Head

It's smart to wear a helmet when you're biking because you could fall off your bike and hit your head. Helmets protect your brain from injury—that's why football players, race car drivers, and construction workers wear them! This poster is a great safety reminder.

| Directions: | Write your request on paper, and put it in an envelope. You must enclose **$1.00.** |
|---|---|
| Write to: | National SAFE KIDS Campaign<br>111 Michigan Avenue, NW<br>Washington, DC 20010-2970 |
| Ask for: | Helmet poster |

# Join the Bucket Brigade

Glue this red, white, and blue label to a one-pound coffee can to make an emergency fire pail. When you fill the can with baking soda, it's ready to put out any electrical or grease fire. You'll also get instructions and a fire chart.

| Directions: | Write your request on paper, and put it in an envelope. You must enclose a long self-addressed, stamped envelope. |
|---|---|
| Write to: | Fire Pail<br>Church & Dwight<br>Arm & Hammer Division<br>P.O. Box 7648-FS94<br>Princeton, NJ 08543-7648 |
| Ask for: | Fire Pail label |

# Lend a Hand

You can make a difference to a kid in a developing country and have fun, too. UNICEF (United Nations Children's Fund) sponsors nutrition, health care, water, education, and emergency relief programs for children in developing countries throughout the world. Send for a famous UNICEF orange collection carton so you can collect donations for UNICEF this Halloween. You'll also get a Halloween safety tips bookmark.

| | |
|---|---|
| **Directions:** | Write your request on paper, and put it in an envelope. You must enclose an 8-by-10-inch self-addressed, stamped envelope with **two 29¢** stamps. |
| **Write to:** | U.S. Committee for UNICEF<br>Group Programs<br>Department 1878P<br>333 East 38th Street<br>New York, NY 10016 |
| **Ask for:** | Trick-or-treat for UNICEF collection carton and safety tips bookmark |

# Helping Grandma

Does someone you love have Alzheimer's disease? This coloring book shows you what happens when a person gets this disease and how loved ones can help.

| **Directions:** | Use a postcard. |
| --- | --- |
| **Write to:** | Sandoz<br>59 Route 10<br>East Hanover, NJ 07936<br>Attention: Mature Market |
| **Ask for:** | Helping Grandma coloring book |

# Helping Each Other

This coloring book teaches you about four serious illnesses that sometimes affect kids and adults. You'll learn about diabetes, epilepsy, mental illness, and hypertension.

| **Directions:** | Use a postcard. |
| --- | --- |
| **Write to:** | Sandoz<br>59 Route 10<br>East Hanover, NJ 07936<br>Attention: Mature Market |
| **Ask for:** | Helping Each Other coloring book |

# Get Healthy

These colorful cartoon sticker sheets show you what you need to do to be a healthy kid. They'll help you remember to eat right, avoid drugs, get lots of exercise, and more! You'll get three sheets.

| | |
|---|---|
| **Directions:** | Write your request on paper, and put it in an envelope. You must enclose **$1.00.** |
| **Write to:** | Special Products Department FS 34 Romeyn Avenue Amsterdam, NY 12010 |
| **Ask for:** | Healthy Kids sticker sheets |

# Safety Counts

Fire drills are not just for school—your family should also practice what to do in case of a fire. These large safety stickers are fun to place on book bags, folders, lunch boxes, and more. You'll get three sheets.

| | |
|---|---|
| **Directions:** | Write your request on paper, and put it in an envelope. You must enclose **$1.00.** |
| **Write to:** | ITG Safety-Smart Stickers P.O. Box 119 Redondo Beach, CA 90277 |
| **Ask for:** | Safety-Smart stickers |

# Just Say No!

What should you do if a friend or stranger offers you drugs? Just say, "No!" and then tell someone you trust about it. These coloring and activity books teach you about the bad drugs that you should stay away from and their effects on your health.

| Directions: | Write your request on paper, and put it in an envelope. You must enclose **$1.00** and **one 29¢** stamp for **each** coloring book you request. (*No checks please.*) |
|---|---|
| **Write to:** | Safe Child<br>P.O. Box 40 1594<br>Brooklyn, NY 11240-1594 |
| **Ask for:** | • Be Smart Say No to Drugs coloring book<br>• Winning Kids Don't Need Drugs coloring book |

# Snuff Is Bad Stuff

Smokeless tobacco, often called "snuff" or "chew," is bad news for kids and adults. It can cause mouth sores, cancer, and even high blood pressure. Learn how to avoid this harmful habit by reading this pamphlet that folds out into a cool poster to hang in your room.

| Directions: | Use a postcard. |
|---|---|
| **Write to:** | Consumer Information Center<br>Department 549Z<br>Pueblo, CO 81009 |
| **Ask for:** | Chew or Snuff pamphlet |

# Take a Deep Breath

You might know that you need your lungs to breathe, but what else do you know about them? The American Lung Association makes learning fun with a coloring book, a crossword puzzle book, and an activity book. Specify which items you want.

| Directions: | Use a postcard. |
|---|---|
| **Write to:** | American Lung Association<br>GPO Box #596-RB<br>New York, NY 10116-0596 |
| **Ask for:** | • **#0840** No Smoking, Lungs at Work activity book<br>• **#0071** Let's Solve the Smokeword puzzle book<br>• **#0043** No Smoking coloring book |

# No Smoking!

When you can't breathe, nothing else matters.® Tell your family and friends that you don't want them to smoke by hanging up this sign that warns: Lungs at Work No Smoking.

| Directions: | Use a postcard. |
|---|---|
| **Write to:** | American Lung Association<br>GPO Box #596-RB<br>New York, NY 10116-0596 |
| **Ask for:** | **#0121** Lungs at Work sign |

# Smoking Isn't Cool

This colorful, action-packed comic book stars the amazing Spider-Man and other superheroes who battle the villain, Smokescreen. Read it, and see how smoking affects your health and life—for the worse.

| **Directions:** | Use a postcard. |
|---|---|
| **Write to:** | Your local American Cancer Society office. It's listed in the telephone book. |
| **Ask for:** | Spider-Man comic book |

# Dealing with Cancer

If someone in your family has cancer, you'll want to read these booklets. They explain what cancer is, what kind of different treatments are available for helping patients, and how to understand the confusing thoughts and feelings you're having. You may request one or both items.

| **Directions:** | Use a postcard. |
|---|---|
| **Write to:** | Your local American Cancer Society office. It's listed in the telephone book. |
| **Ask for:** | • When Your Brother or Sister Has Cancer booklet<br>• When Mom or Dad Has Cancer booklet |

# Tin Grins Are In!

You can learn all about orthodontics and wearing braces from this newsletter and these two pamphlets. You may request one or more items.

| Directions: | Use a postcard. |
|---|---|
| **Write to:** | American Association of Orthodontists Department KD 401 North Lindbergh Boulevard St. Louis, MO 63141-7816 |
| **Ask for:** | • 'Smiles' newsletter • Facts about Orthodontics pamphlet • Careers in Orthodontics pamphlet |

# Speak Silently

You can talk without making a sound. It's no trick with sign language. Many speech- and hearing-impaired people learn how to communicate using the same manual alphabet you'll get on this card and button.

**INTERPRETER CARD
MANUAL ALPHABET**

| Directions: | Write your request on paper, and put it in an envelope. You must enclose a long self-addressed, stamped envelope and **$1.00.** |
|---|---|
| **Write to:** | Keep Quiet P.O. Box 361 Stanhope, NJ 07874 |
| **Ask for:** | Manual alphabet card and button |

# Jolly Good Time

You can make a perfect popcorn ball without burning your fingers or getting them sticky. Send for this red plastic popcorn ball maker—it's a fun and tasty activity!

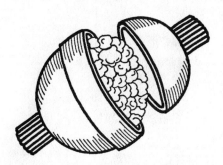

| | |
|---|---|
| **Directions:** | Write your request on paper, and put it in an envelope. You must enclose **$1.00.** |
| **Write to:** | Jolly Time Pop Corn<br>American Pop Corn Company<br>P. O. Box 178, Department H<br>Sioux City, IA 51102 |
| **Ask for:** | Jolly Time Pop Corn Ball Maker |

# Rice Is Nice

Learn how climate and terrain combine to produce top-quality rice in many U.S. states. Send for more facts about rice and a pamphlet of low-fat recipes. You may request one or more items.

| | |
|---|---|
| **Directions:** | Write your request on paper, and put it in an envelope. You must enclose a long self-addressed, stamped envelope for **each** item you request. |
| **Write to:** | The Rice Council<br>P.O. Box 740121<br>Houston, TX 77274 |
| **Ask for:** | • Facts about U.S. Rice pamphlet<br>• Light, Lean, and Low-Fat Recipes pamphlet<br>• Teaching the Fun Way. . .with Rice! booklet |

# Emergency!

Do you know what to do if you're involved in an emergency? These sixteen-page coloring and activity books explain first aid, calling 911, and what it's like to go to the emergency room. They include mazes, dot-to-dots, and award certificates that show that you know what to do in a real emergency.

| | |
|---|---|
| **Directions:** | Write your request on paper, and put it in an envelope. You must enclose **$1.00** and **one 29¢** stamp for **each** coloring book you request. (*No checks please.*) |
| **Write to:** | Safe Child<br>P.O. Box 40 1594<br>Brooklyn, NY 11240-1594 |
| **Ask for:** | • A Visit to the Emergency Center coloring book<br>• In an Emergency Dial 911 coloring book<br>• Know Emergency First Aid coloring book |

# INDEX

# INDEX

**The Free Stuff Editors**
Meadowbrook Press
Deephaven, MN 55391

1994 EDITION

U.S. MAIL

# MORE FREE STUFF FOR KIDS

**Hundreds of free and up-to-a-dollar***
**things kids can send for by mail!**

*Plus some extra-special values!

If you're a big fan of *Free Stuff for Kids,* you'll love *More Free Stuff for Kids!* It's filled with hundreds of offers, including basketball fan packs, stickers, writing supplies, holiday stuff, save the animals info, multicultural items, cool jewelry, and more.

Look in your favorite bookstore or order from **Meadowbrook Press.**

Kids can order a *free* catalog featuring all of Meadowbrook's kids' books!

**Write to:** Meadowbrook, Inc.
18318 Minnetonka Boulevard
Deephaven, MN 55391

# Order Form

| Quantity | Title | Author | Order No. | Unit Cost | Total |
|---|---|---|---|---|---|
| | Almost Grown-Up | Patterson, Claire | 2290 | $4.95 | |
| | Dads Say the Dumbest Things! | Lansky/Jones | 4220 | $6.00 | |
| | Dino Dots | Dixon, Dougal | 2250 | $4.95 | |
| | Free Stuff for Kids, 1994 edition | Free Stuff Editors | 2190 | $5.00 | |
| | Grandma Knows Best | McBride, Mary | 4009 | $5.00 | |
| | Hocus Pocus Stir & Cook, Kitchen Science | Lewis, James | 2380 | $7.00 | |
| | How To Embarrass Your Kids | Holleman/Sherins | 4005 | $6.00 | |
| | Kids Pick the Funniest Poems | Lansky, Bruce | 2410 | $13.00 | |
| | Learn While You Scrub, Science in the Tub | Lewis, James | 2350 | $7.00 | |
| | Measure Pour & Mix, Kitchen Science Tricks | Lewis, James | 2370 | $7.00 | |
| | Moms Say the Funniest Things! | Lansky, Bruce | 4280 | $6.00 | |
| | More Free Stuff for Kids, 1994 edition | Free Stuff Editors | 2191 | $5.00 | |
| | New Adventures of Mother Goose | Lansky, Bruce | 2420 | $15.00 | |
| | Rub-a-Dub-Dub, Science in the Tub | Lewis, James | 2270 | $6.00 | |
| | Sand Castles Step-by-Step | Wierenga/McDonald | 2300 | $6.95 | |
| | Webster's Dictionary Game | Webster, Wilbur | 6030 | $5.95 | |
| | Weird Wonders and Bizarre Blunders | Schreiber, Brad | 4120 | $4.95 | |
| | | | | Subtotal | |
| | | | Shipping and Handling (see below) | | |
| | | | MN residents add 6.5% sales tax | | |
| | | | | Total | |

**YES,** please send me the books indicated above. Add $2.00 shipping and handling for the first book and $.50 for each additional book. Add $2.50 to total for books shipped to Canada. Overseas postage will be billed. Allow up to 4 weeks for delivery. Send check or money order payable to Meadowbrook Press. No cash or C.O.D.'s, please. Prices subject to change without notice. **Quantity discounts available upon request.**

Send book(s) to:

Name _____ Phone _____

Address _____

City _____ State _____ Zip_____

**Payment via:**

❑ Check or money order payable to Meadowbrook Press. (No cash or C.O.D.'s, please.) Amount enclosed $ _____
❑ Visa (for orders over $10.00 only)    ❑ MasterCard (for orders over $10.00 only)
    Account # _____ Signature _____ Exp. Date _____

**A FREE Meadowbrook Press catalog is available upon request.**
*You can also phone us for orders of $10.00 or more at 1-800-338-2232.*
**Mail to:** Meadowbrook, Inc., 18318 Minnetonka Blvd., Deephaven, MN 55391
Toll-Free 1-800-338-2232

(612) 473-5400                                                    FAX (612) 475-0736